Staffordshire Bull Terriers

JOHN F. GORDON

With line drawings by
CAROLINE WOODALL

FOYLES HANDBOOKS
LONDON

First published 1964
Reprinted 1969
Reprinted 1970
Reprinted 1973
Reprinted 1976

Published in Great Britain by
W. & G. Foyle Ltd.,
125 Charing Cross Road,
London WC2H 0EB

Printed and bound in Great Britain by
Redwood Burn Limited
Trowbridge & Esher

Contents

List of Illustrations

CHAPTER ONE

Origin and History

SOME eight or nine varieties of dogs come within the general classification of Bull Breeds. All lay claim to the Bulldog as a common ancestor, which when crossed with certain other breeds and developed by careful selection according to the use or fancy required of them, produced these different and distinct sorts. One such breed is the Staffordshire Bull Terrier, which as his name implies is a product of the Bulldog and one or more from the Terrier group.

Were we of such a mind we could probe back far into history to establish the variety and form of the Bulldog's early progenitors. However, the purpose of this little book is to cover rather the development of the Staffordshire Bull Terrier than to delve too patiently into early and extinct forms like the Molossus which existed in Greece thousands of years ago. Nevertheless, the Bulldog has played a very important part in canine history. He is accepted as a national breed in this country, and as the vital ingredient in the manufacture of the Staffordshire Bull Terrier he deserves at least more than a casual glance at his background.

The Bulldog and Mastiff are closely linked in the past. Some will have it that at one time they were as one breed and parted their ways centuries ago to develop along distinct and separate lines. Certainly, they are related intimately among the short-faced group of dogs and they or a kind of dog closely approximating to them were known in Great Britain as early as at the beginning of the Christian era.

From whence they came is uncertain, but the belief that the Phoenicians imported them to Britain well before this time would appear reasonable. Certainly, by the time the Romans landed here such dogs were well established and domiciled. We are told in early times that the Ancient Britons took with them into battle against the Roman invaders, large, ferocious and formidable dogs of ugly countenance. Undoubtedly such dogs, the war-dogs, were ancestors of the present day Bulldog and his more modern off-shoot, the Staffordshire Bull Terrier. That these animals were of supreme courage and effective in battle is evident from the fact that many were shipped back to Italy. There they were used in arena sports and pitted against armed men and wild beasts — pastimes at which it is understood they showed considerable prowess.

From Italy, many of these dogs found their way to other lands in Southern Europe. There in union with divers native breeds they produced and eventually influenced a number of breeds we accept to-day as pure-bred varieties, heavily built and short-faced kinds such as the St. Bernard of Switzerland and the Bullenbeiser of ancient Germany, progenitor of the modern Boxer. In France, where the English Court was held for some time during the twelfth century, large numbers of these dogs were acquired to regale the royal functions with baiting sports. Writers of the day describe them as being possessed with exceptional courage and tenacity, huge in head and short-muzzled. There they were known as Alaunts and from the Alaunt descended the great fighting dog of France, the Dogue de Bordeaux.

Although the dubious sports of baiting the bear and other large animals can be traced back to the days of the Norman Conquest, enthusiasm for these practices never waxed so high as in the time of our Elizabethan forefathers.

In this era dogs were named according to their function or appearance. Names such as the 'Keeper', 'Watchman', 'Butchers Dogge' are examples. Dr. John Caius in his *De Canibus Britannicis,* 1570, describes a dog, almost certainly the Mastiff or Bulldog — '. . . an huge dogge, stubborne, eager, burthenous of body and therefore of but little swiftness, terrible and fearful to behold and more fearse and fell than any Arcadian curr'. Caius groups this animal and other 'functional' breeds under one heading *Canes Rustici* or dogs of the country. They are referred to as Mastives, a word suggestive of large breeds but in those days descriptive of curs, although not with the same derogatory implication as in modern usage. Again, all the dogs used at the baiting sports and as guards were of necessity big ones of considerable girth and substance. To them the old English word 'masty' meaning 'fat' would have been applied and perhaps later corrupted to the name Mastiff covering *all* such dogs of these functions. Certainly, from such a family of dogs would the Bulldog have been developed although he would not have been named Bulldog until the firm establishment of the sport of Bull-baiting. In this he was to take a vital and prominent part.

Although cursory mention is made of Bull-baiting four centuries before the Elizabethan period, its hey-day as a sport was undoubtedly during the sixteenth century. Bear-baiting had begun to lose vogue. It had to be conducted in a more confined space than was essential for Bull-baiting. It was a slower sport and no doubt entailed less 'gate-money' for the promoters to whom the more extravagant spectacle of Bull-baiting opened up greater possibilities. However, this 'new' sport did need a faster dog than hitherto. Consequently, the 100 — 120 lb. animal gave way to a small, more agile edition of his kind, a dog of some ninety lb. weight which lacked nothing in the courage and ferocious tenacity of his forerunner.

In this revolting sport the dog was expected to pin the

bull by its nose to the ground, maintaining his hold meanwhile. To approach the bull and take hold he had to move
in low and fast with one eye on the larger animal's horns.
If he was careless he stood to be impaled or tossed high
in the air only to be shattered when he hit the ground.
Some were fortunate enough though, to be caught in their
owners' capacious aprons or slid down a long staff to safety
before they reached destruction in this way. It became
necessary then to produce a dog rather shorter in the leg,
certainly lower to ground than before and a somewhat
closer coupled, more squat animal was bred. This came a
little nearer in type at least to the Bulldog we know to-day.

The Bear Gardens and open places on the South Bank
of the Thames became popular meeting places for the
lovers of the sport and these places were patronised in the
same manner as a football fixture would be supported
to-day. The influence of the sport and its thrill spread to
many provincial towns and even to-day some public squares
and places bear the name 'Bull Ring' and similar indications of the cruel pastime which held such early sway in
the land. Its popularity became such that on occasions
events got out of hand with impromptu baits at Bank
Holiday Fairs. The authorities had little success in their
spasmodic efforts to stem these sports and it was not until
1835 when the Humane Act was passed that baiting sports
and the rather lesser-known but possibly crueller sport of
dog-fighting were abolished. At least, such was the intention
of the Act and although it was instrumental in halting the
baitings, it was not so easy to stop dog-fighting which now
came into its own, in spite of the law. It was a sport which
could be carried on in any cellar or hole-and-corner venue.
To avoid the law was relatively easy therefore, and indeed
in many mining areas dog-fighting was carried on more or
less openly, and a Sunday morning out, with a full
programme of dog-fighting, cock-fighting, and finishing up
with some bare-knuckle bouts, was common.

At the start of the nineteenth century dog pits were springing up everywhere. It was a fashionable sport not only with the seamy section of the populace but patronised in no small measure by the aristocracy who would enjoy wagering the outcome of a match between two celebrated dogs in a fight to the death. London had its notorious pit in Duck Lane, Westminster and here a regulation pit was maintained. Dogs were matched weight for weight and matches were controlled by rules which remained unchanged and were rigidly enforced for over 100 years. Crafty attempts to sabotage a contestant by rubbing some obnoxious concoction into his adversary's coat were seldom successful at such a place although similar ruses may well have got by at matches which were less well managed. At the Duck Lane pit considerable sums were won and lost. Winning dogs achieved great fame and were sold for sums which would put to shame some of the prices taken for modern show dogs. Occasionally 'kinky' battles would be staged and it is on record that one such bout featured a dog matched against a monkey, the simian being provided with a metal bar which he used as a club on the dog's head! It was a sport in which gameness was a by-word. No other creed was wanted in a dog except this, but again, he had to be faster. The bear-baiter had given way in size to the bull-baiting dog, and now the latter was too big for dog-fighting. Thus a smaller, faster, determined dog, full of courage and fire, appeared on the scene. He was needed to fight and kill and never give way. Breeders turned to the process of making such a dog and although their methods were perhaps diverse in the early stages their ultimate production was a dog we now know as the Staffordshire Bull Terrier.

The actual method of manufacture of this dog is rather clouded. Suffice to say early crossings with the Bulldog and a small active Terrier took place about 150 years ago. The suggestive names 'Bulldog-Terrier', 'Bull-and-Terrier' and

finally 'Bull Terrier' give evidence of such a union. Which
Terrier was used in the union is indeterminate. The
Bulldog of the day, that is the breed which existed here
around the start of the nineteenth century was a dog with
cleaner lines than we accept to-day. He would have weighed
however, some sixty lb. for the smaller kind of Bulldog
would have received preference in such a breeding scheme.
This dog was crossed with a small native Terrier, short-
coated and perhaps twenty lb. in weight. The Terrier
family is a large one, being an immense concourse of all
sorts of Terriers and types of Terriers from the common
material of the land. It is a family of considerable antiquity
and although no doubt many and varied were the kinds
put to the Bulldog it would seem that the main lot in the
union fell to the Old English Terrier. This breed is extinct
now but it is an important one in history. Not only did
this tough little Terrier prove instrumental in the production of the Staffordshire but he was progenitor of other
indigenous breeds such as the Old English Black-and-Tan
Terrier, later to be known as the Manchester Terrier. Stock
which came from the union of the Bulldog and this Terrier
would have varied in extreme cases at maturity between
twenty and sixty lb. weight, averaging no doubt between
thirty and forty-five lb. This weight margin allowed a
dog which was substantial, muscular and athletic. These
attributes motivated with courage and tenacity produced
fighting dogs for over 100 years and gave us the Staffordshire
Bull Terrier. Our breed's forerunner appeared in a variety
of coat colours — reds, fawns, brindles of many shades and
any of these colours with white. White dogs and black-and-
tans were not uncommon with liver-coloured specimens,
although the two last-mentioned colours are not approved
in the modern show world.

The old Pit Bull Terrier, the dog we call the Staffordshire
Bull Terrier to-day, gave us the all-white English Bull
Terrier. This was formed around the 1860's in Birmingham

by James Hinks. He crossed the original dog with the Old English White Terrier, now extinct and possible sundry other breeds predominately white. Soon after the turn of the current century, the all-white, fashionable Bull Terrier was crossed back to the Pit Bull Terrier and a coloured variety of the former kind was evolved, being named the Coloured Bull Terrier. Unfortunately for the Pit Bull Terrier, these breeds had the advantage over him in the matter of title. Being the original Bull Terrier he should have had prior claim to that name. However, his existence through the nineteenth century had been obscure, and he had an evil reputation because of his fighting prowess. He was never considered as a show dog, unlike his all-white cousin which received Kennel Club blessing with the coming of the dog shows in the last quarter of the last century. With this acceptance the all-white was named 'Bull Terrier' and our own breed lost the prerogative of the name to which he is by right entitled. However, it was not until 1935, due to the representations to The Kennel Club by a small band of enthusiasts, that he was accepted to the Registry of that august body as a pure-bred variety, under the title Staffordshire Bull Terrier. As it happens, his admirers these days have no quarrel with the name, for he was virtually evolved in the Black Country, the mining area of South Staffordshire and it is felt the dog has a proud and traditional title, which as a native breed suits him and which he deserves.

CHAPTER TWO

Basic Strains
and Bloodlines

I T W A S a difficult task to convince some of the dog-fighting
fraternity that their beloved Pit Bull Terrier — and it
is true, these men did love their dogs even though they
treated them so appallingly — should be given the opportunity of sitting on a show bench and become eligible
for exhibition. The pioneers, those breeders who believed
such a grand dog deserved a better existence, fought for his
rights and eventually a few classes at minor shows were
staged. As might be expected from a dog bred at the time
to fight or at least to possess the temperament and
characteristics of a fighter, such events were frequently
turned into melées. Naturally, such happenings did little
to improve the status of the breed or to endear it to show-
goers with less pugnacious varieties. However, matters
became better organised by the enthusiasts and gradually
the Staffordshire Bull Terrier came into his own.

One of the first events at which the breed attended was a
modest four-class Exemption show in Cradley Heath, S.
Staffs., in 1935. The judge Mr. F. W. Holden, who is to-day
well-known in the breed as a successful producer of winners,
was asked to judge the show and to give four placings to
Staffords, quite apart from any official win they might
sustain. The Terrier class was judged and Mr. Birch's
'Monty', later to be registered 'Vindictive Monty' won, with
Mr. Shaw's 'Jim' ('Jim the Dandy') second, the third and
fourth placings to Pegg's 'Joe' ('Fearless Joe') and Mallen's

'Cross Guns Johnson' respectively. At the show twenty-six dogs paraded, many of these proving vital links with the old dogs of un-written pedigree and those who were destined to prove the pillars of scientific pedigree breeding.

With the success of this and later ventures, the breed went from strength to strength and adherents made every effort to popularise it. Two of the early winners, already referred to — 'Fearless Joe' and 'Jim the Dandy' were regarded as among the best of their day and both were in fact held in mind as ideal type when the breed Standard was prepared. The original Standard, which will be discussed in a later chapter was argued on at length, but was finally adopted by a general meeting of the newly formed Staffordshire Bull Terrier Club on 15th June, 1935. The Club, which is to-day fondly referred to as the 'Parent' Club set the key-stone in the progress of the Staffordshire. It gave the dog a status in Dogdom and instead of the onetime sidelong glance or even a sneer he may have received from the owners of perhaps more lordly breeds he was treated with respect. Admittedly, much of this respect may well have been fearful respect, but now at least the breed was receiving notice.

The first official show held by the Club was on the bowling green of the Cradley Heath Conservative Club, 17th August 1935 with Mr. H. N. Beilby judging. A large entry of more than sixty paraded and 'Jim the Dandy' won the day. It was an honour for Mr. Beilby to judge this memorial event, but then Mr. Beilby was destined to make some outstanding services to the breed. He went into the pedigrees of the various Staffordshire Bull Terrier strains based on the 'Line and Family' method, following the example of the late Rev. Rosslyn Bruce whose efforts on similar lines had been so successful with Smooth Fox Terriers. From his findings he published a number of genealogical charts, and later distinct lines for the various strains. Six Lines, (A line is the sire's male ancestors, i.e.

sire's sire's sire) were evolved, these being known as the M, J, L. R, B and C Lines. In the early days each line assumed an individual and distinct importance and developed accordingly. However, in the passing years some lines have waned and currently the M-Line is pre-eminent with the J and R Lines some way behind. The M Line has led, in fact, for many years, due no doubt to the successful use at stud of the immortal Ch. Gentleman Jim. This great piebald dog was born in 1937 and lived for twelve years. He was the sire of over 250 registered Staffordshire Bull Terriers at a time when the breed was enjoying a boom following upon the war-starved years. He continued siring stock up to the age of ten years and it is clear that his influence must have been immense.

The bitch Families, of which more than sixty were established were maintained on paper for many years. A Family is the dam's female ancestors, i.e. dam's dam's dam. These became somewhat unwieldy in form and I am not sure whether there is any up-to-date material available to the student to-day, unlike the Lines which have been tabulated with care up to the present and contain much useful material for the serious breeder.

CHAPTER THREE

The Standard
and the Judge

F ROM 1935 when the breed Standard was evolved,
breeders have been promising themselves the Perfect
Staffordshire Bull Terrier. On occasions certain specimens
have been hailed as or near to that ideal. Unfortunately,
the opinions of the claimants have necessarily been dis-
counted, more or less according to the surfeit of their
ill-judged enthusiasm. Admittedly, many great dogs have
been bred in the last quarter-century, some of them quite
close to the perfect state. That these still left some margin
for improvement to the ideal is generally agreed upon and
to date, in common with most other breeds, the embodi-
ment of a perfect Staffordshire Bull Terrier has yet to
appear.

No doubt every judge hopes that one day a perfect dog
will appear before him and that his opinion as the finder
of this paragon will be endorsed by other expert judges
of the breed. Oddly enough however, the opinion of judges,
even the experienced and expert ones, is seldom synonymous, although at times where really good dogs are
concerned the variation is slight. Of course, if every judge
thought the same and the same dog won every time and
placings were identical show after show, the hobby of
exhibiting dogs would soon die a natural death. Variety
and difference of opinion and the interpretation of the
breed Standard make for interest in the game. Exhibitors
travel considerable distances to get individual opinion and

it is seldom that a good dog does not get his just deserts. Judges may not think exactly the same, but proper and correct judging ends showing only slight variations in assessment. These margins of opinion are necessary, even essential in maintaining the steady pulse of dog showing.

An experienced judge has owned, bred or seen a lot of good dogs. Many of these dogs have been celebrated pillars of the breed. A *good* judge retains in his thoughts the best and most favourable features of every great dog. He endeavours to *create* in his 'mind's eye' a picture of the Perfect Staffordshire Bull Terrier. This perfect specimen is one therefore, which has borrowed from the best dogs their best features. One day, no doubt, this Olympian will appear. For the moment, we can only be patient and hope.

In 1948 (9th October), The Staffordshire Bull Terrier Clubs' Advisory Council, now defunct, recommended certain amendments to the original breed Standard. The suggested revision was eventually accepted by The Kennel Club, becoming official in January, 1950. The Standard of the Staffordshire Bull Terrier is reproduced herewith by kind permission of The Kennel Club and following upon the individual sections is my own comment as to its suggested interpretation. The sketches can be referred to in conjunction with these remarks and may act as a visual guide to the would-be judge. He should remember, however, that although each section of the Standard has its *individual* importance, his final judgment must rest upon a satisfactory fusing of the points or moulding of the ingredients into the dog as a *whole*.

Perhaps my exhortations in the ensuing pages on the subject of the Staffordshire's fighting potential may give rise to the thought that I endorse, even support, the so-called sport of dog-fighting. Nothing could be further from the truth. It is a degrading pastime and one to which I am strongly opposed. However, the Staffordshire Bull Terrier was bred for it and his characteristic conformation and temperament developed solely with fighting in mind. Consequently, as a show dog now, he needs to be judged on the basis of his physical requirements as a fighting dog as should another breed be judged physically characteristic to its specific function in life.

Characteristics

From the past history of the Staffordshire Bull Terrier, the modern dog draws his character of indomitable courage, high intelligence and tenacity. This coupled with his affection for his friends, and children in particular, his off-duty quietness and trustworthy stability, makes him the foremost all-purpose dog.

Such points of character are not easy to assess in a dog at which you may be looking for the first time. They are intangibles. Certainly, you will be aware if a dog is aggressive, composed or shy, but as to his true character you can do little more than surmise, unless you know him intimately. Some people think a snarling, mouthy dog is a game one. Often, the opposite is true and many dogs exhibit in this way only because they feel safe with their owner at the other end of the lead! Obviously, such a dog does not conform to this section of the Standard, but how do you assess him? In judging Characteristics, your yard-stick is largely one of commonsense, coupled with your knowledge of the breed.

LOOK FOR: A keen, intelligent eye, a-glint and with obvious awareness. The stance should be poised and indicative of readiness, the dog up on his toes. The tail should be controlled, not slack and the body vibratory in energetic outline. You should observe exhibition spirit too — an attribute coupled to the main section and this allows a dog to show himself to advantage, enjoying the show game. Such state of mind can help a dog to the top even against others better in quality than he, but who lack enjoyment of the show ring.

General appearance

The Staffordshire Bull Terrier is a smooth-coated dog. He should be of great strength for his size and although muscular should be active and agile.

The general appearance of a dog can do much for him. Many judges take their first impressions from the dogs as they enter the ring to be judged. Sometimes a judge will mentally pick his ultimate winner of the class even before

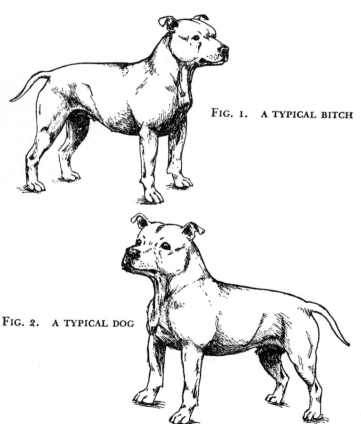

FIG. 1.   A TYPICAL BITCH

FIG. 2.   A TYPICAL DOG

he has handled it! Of course, some latent fault may be revealed after handling which would necessitate a change of mind, but there is no doubt that a dog with bold, classical outlines, amply laden with breed type and with his component parts moulded smoothly into a pleasing picture can stand out well from his fellows.

LOOK FOR: Excellent show condition, a fine glistening natural coat. Good clean bone and frame structure with the blending of each body department into a well balanced specimen, adequately endowed with breed type. Breed type is that quality essential to a dog if he is to have pleasing balance between correct anatomical structure and general appearance. Individual type is expressed more by points and detail.

Head and Skull

Short, deep through, broad skull, very pronounced cheek muscles, distinct stop, short foreface, black nose.

In his head and skull you see the hall-mark and typical rugged beauty of the true Staffordshire Bull Terrier. The strong broad, short muzzle and bumpy cheek muscles are in effect the visual and basic conception of the Stafford as a fighting dog. The original Scale of Points, not in use these

FIG. 3.   HEAD STUDIES

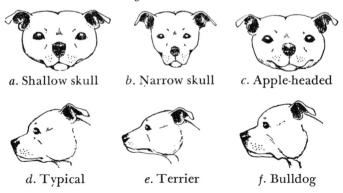

a. Shallow skull   b. Narrow skull   c. Apple-headed

d. Typical   e. Terrier   f. Bulldog

days, allocated Head and Skull thirty per cent of the total points. This was later reduced to a quarter of the whole, but it indicates the importance with which these components were regarded.

LOOK FOR: A solid, blocky, muscular head of great breadth and depth. It has been stated that an ideal balance for skull and muzzle is in ratio of 2 : 1 respectively (see Fig. 3 d). This is endorsed. Big, black nostrils are desirable in a fighting dog who would need sustaining deep breath in battle. Jet black noses are a guide to sound pigmentation. Do not be misled into giving favours to a doggy-headed bitch, however tempting she may prove. A bitch should look feminine. If she is doggy in appearance it is a fault, although not as bad as a dog which lacks masculinity. Admittedly, sometimes such bitches are useful in a breeding programme which needs to improve heads, but their employment needs expert knowledge and some caution. In the show ring she should take second place to a bitch of equal merit elsewhere but with a head styled in feminine lines. Ensure considerable breadth across the top of the muzzle where it joins the skull and here should be a well defined stop, the indentation between and in front of the eyes. The shape of the muzzle and formation and development of the jaw muscles in a fighting dog are of obvious importance, so make sure the muzzle is deep and strong. Look at the repandus, bent upward part of the underjaw. This should be plainly visible when viewed from the side, neither shallow nor receding.

Eyes

Dark preferable but may bear some relation to coat colour. Round, of medium size, and set to look straight ahead.

You will not get correct Staffordshire Bull Terrier expression unless the colour, size and emplacement of the eyes are correct. Each attribute plays its part to this end.

The eyes, they say, are windows to the human soul. It is true in the case of dogs, too. You can often tell a Staffordshire Bull Terrier's character by looking into his eyes, but do not stare too intently as the real sort seldom like it!

LOOK FOR: Keen, rather glinting eyes and a distinct awareness. It is said that colour may bear some relation to the coat, but in my opinion, dark brown eyes are better in a part-Terrier breed than pale eyes. The former usually indicate intelligence as opposed to shrewdness in the latter. Do not tolerate dogs with bulbous or protruding eyes. Apart from the vapid, atypical expression they bestow, in a fighting dog such an eye would be vulnerable.

Ears

Rose or half-pricked and not large. Full drop or prick to be penalised.

Ears play an important part in general appearance. Ears should be carried alertly. Badly carried ears and big ears detract from the pleasurable appreciation of a Staffordshire Bull Terrier. The medium sized rose ear is superior to other kinds. If a dog has half-pricked ears, they need to be

FIG. 4.   EAR STUDIES

a. Typical 'rose'   *b*. Semi-erect   *c*. Erect   *d*. Button

small and perky in use to equal rose ears. Such appendages are frequently thick in cartilage at the point where they join the skull, causing rigidity.

LOOK FOR: Supple, medium texture in the ears which should be small to medium in size. It is important that they should be tidy. A fighting dog of the old days would be at a grave disadvantage with big, thick ears which any adversary could easily seize and hold. Small rose ears are easily folded outward and back and tucked away behind the swell of the skull out of harm's way. It is this type of ear which must receive favour in judging.

Mouth

The mouth should be level, that is, the incisors of the lower jaw should fit closely inside the incisors of the top jaw and the lips should be tight and clean. The badly undershot or overshot mouth to be heavily penalised.

In a breed whose Standard demands a short foreface, there exists a tendency to 'lippiness' in some strains. This looseness of skin around the mouth would open up considerable advantages to a biting adversary so we have to breed dogs with tight, clean lips and judges need to condemn those which do not conform. You are told by the Standard that a badly undershot or overshot mouth should be heavily penalised, but be sure that before you heed the word 'heavy' you understand the word 'badly'. In judging

FIG. 5.   MUZZLES

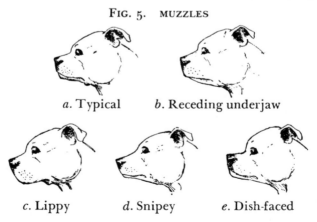

a. Typical   *b.* Receding underjaw

c. Lippy   *d.* Snipey   *e.* Dish-faced

the Staffordshire Bull Terrier with either of these faults be sure you penalise according to its severity. A *badly* undershort or overshot mouth is one with a distinctly visible gap or channel between the upper and lower incisors or front teeth. You would see this when you lifted the dog's lips to examine his mouth, although it may be stated that often a badly undershot dog's fault is apparent even with his mouth closed. These are critical faults and may be penalised at your discretion. However, if the mouth is only slightly out of line, then although a fault, it does not justify the heavy penalties that some judges impose. Slightly undershot mouths (you do not come across the overshot variety much these days) are faults comparable only to such as bad formation of ears, gay tails and tight shoulders and should be faulted accordingly.

I have seen dogs good enough in type and conformation to beat all present in the show ring denied the privilege of a prize solely because of a slightly undershot mouth, a fault which the judge had amplified out of all proportion to its severity. You will be told that such mouths are transmittable faults in breeding. True, but then so are the other faults I have mentioned as are almost all physical and temperamental deficiencies. I do not support bad mouths, far from that, but I do believe that a judge's opinion should be fairly balanced. I have seen too many good dogs condemned because the judge could not see further than the mouth. Of course, the good dog with a level mouth has the advantage over the good undershot one, not only in the show ring, but more vitally, in combat. A dog strikes down or sideways to bite and when connected he needs to cut with a clean scissor-like action of the teeth. The level mouthed dog can achieve this, the undershot one only with lucky positioning or not at all. His hold can bruise, and the grip is inferior to that of the dog with a level mouth.

LOOK FOR: Tight, clean lips. This attribute is easy enough to find on long muzzled dogs or those with snipey forefaces, but as both forms of muzzle conformation are untenable the value of clean lips is slight. Many short-faced dogs have reasonably clean lips so watch for these and endeavour to average efficiently in your assessment. When you examine a mouth, ensure the teeth are big and strong. Small, close-knit teeth are neither typical nor useful in the Staffordshire Bull Terrier. Remember what has been said about the simple or slightly undershot mouth. If you fault on mouths then reserve your more severe penalties for the *badly* undershot and overshot mouths, wry mouths and flush mouths. The wry mouth is one in which some of the teeth in the top row criss-cross with others in the bottom row. A flush mouth is when the front teeth of both lower and upper rows meet tip to tip. It will be seen that neither of these forms, the wry and flush mouths are acceptable for they do not represent cutting actions in biting and both are inferior to the slightly undershot variety.

Neck

Muscular, rather short, clean in outline and gradually widening towards the shoulders.

A good head should have a powerful, muscular neck to support and administer it. A powerful armament, such as a typical Staffordshire head represents, is of no value without the steel spring that a strong neck can emulate, to direct its action. An overlong neck lacks strength. One which is too short carries loose skin and dewlap. Both extremes ruin the visual balance of a dog when viewed from front and side. Both indicate weakness in physical activity.

Look for: Clean, smooth, muscular neckline. Conformation should be strong, with distinct muscular arch from occiput to point of entry at shoulders with appreciable widening at this area.

Forequarters

Legs straight and well-boned, set rather wide apart, without looseness at the shoulders, and showing no weakness at the pasterns, from which point the feet turn out a little.

It is necessary for the forelegs of the Staffordshire to be set rather wide apart to allow ample chest development. The whole front should be indicative of great muscular development and obvious strength. Balance of the specimen under review is just as important and just as easily assessed from the front as from the side. Here the emphasis is on length of leg and a leggy dog is certainly not a balanced one. An ultra short-legged specimen is inclined to forfeit agility, so we have to ensure our dog does not sacrifice any athletic advantages for solidity. This means that again we have to average in judging for exaggerations in any show specimen are not to be recommended, even though they may be exaggerations of good points, for these make no pretty picture of the breed Standard.

FIG. 6.   FRONT VIEWS

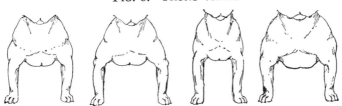

a. Typical   *b.* Out at elbows *c.* Tight front *d.* Bulldog front

LOOK FOR: Good straight lines in front, broken only by the feet turning out a little at the pasterns. Ensure that the elbows do not turn out, for elbows made like this constitute a bad fault. Do not be impressed by 'bossy' shoulders, that is, shoulders with tight, bunchy muscle. This might be a strong muscle, but it is not a lasting one and is a distinct deterrent to clean, easy, forward movement and detracts from the general design of the dog. A long, well toned muscle is preferable and endures longer. By examining the dog's fore parts you can assess correct length of leg and the thickness and roundness of the bone, which by the way, should be ample, rather than heavy. A stilted action in the dog's forward movement may indicate indifferent shoulder emplacement. A shoulder blade which is too perpendicular is said to be 'proppy' and constitutes a fault in forward body structure. Dew claws can be left on the forelegs at an owner's discretion. In the old days these appendages were useful weapons to a breed of dog which would frequently 'wrestle' his opponent in the opening gambit of a bout. I have found that they are seldom troublesome on a Staffordshire Bull Terrier with his fore limbs widely spaced.

Body

The body should be close coupled, with a level topline, wide front, deep brisket and well-sprung ribs, being rather light in the loins.

The body of a Staffordshire must show to even the casual observer, great strength for its size and considerable springiness in body structure. A deep brisket, neck to chest region, should have no evidence of pinching, and the chest itself should be profound. Viewed in profile, the line of chest in an animal of good contour would run through the point of elbow. Massive shoulders without loaded muscle are essential to his powerful make-up and the same applies to a big rib cage, protective framework for a great heart and adequate respiratory machinery. The ribs should shorten as they approach the loin, producing a moderate tuck-up. The sides and loins need to be well filled out, but with muscle, not fat. Fatness is anathema in a Staffordshire Bull Terrier and should be considered seriously against the dog by any judge who admires the breed.

LOOK FOR: A good level topline and compact couplings, that part of the body between the last ribs and hip-joints, connected by the backbone. Try and imagine the dog fitted into a square. If he fits nicely, he is sure to be compact and well balanced which is in his favour. Keep an eye open

FIG. 7.   BODY OUTLINES

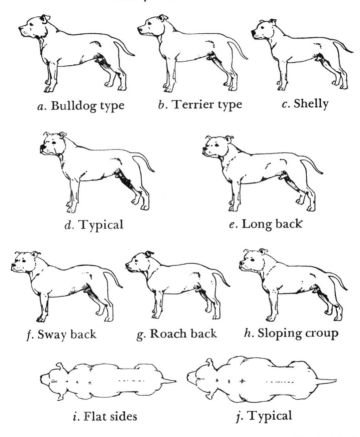

a. Bulldog type   *b*. Terrier type   *c*. Shelly

d. Typical   *e*. Long back

f. Sway back   *g*. Roach back   *h*. Sloping croup

i. Flat sides   *j*. Typical

for the bad sway back. This is evidenced by a dip behind the shoulders, due to poor rib development. The roach back is shown by a convex backline, commencing from a dip at the withers to another at the tail set-on. This is an objectionable fault in the breed, and is due to abnormal arching of the spine, often accompanied by proppy shoulders.

Hindquarters

The hindquarters should be well muscled, hocks let down with stifles well bent. Legs should be parallel when viewed from behind.

An old fighting Staffordshire would not have got very far in combat without well developed hindquarters. Shortness between the point of hock and the foot is essential for adequate spring in action and movement. An attacking dog needs powerful hindquarters to push in at his adversary. Some of the early pit dogs were clever — they knew that once they could take hold of the other dog's stifle and crush it that the animal would be virtually out of the fight, for his propelling machinery would be rendered inoperative. Hindquarters control a dog's dynamic activity and the

FIG. 8.   HINDQUARTERS

a. Typical   *b.* Cow-hocked   *c.* In-toed

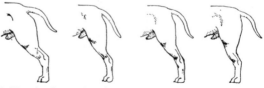

d. Typical   *e.* Straight   *f.* Long   *g.* Set-under
             stifle   straight   hock
                             hock

well bent stifles with well developed second thighs allows him to straighten the hind limb from the state of angulation into the state of complete extension, with maximum

2. (*Below*) Clarke's 'Prince', taken in 1913 when a Stafford was virtually an unknown breed in the south of England.

1. The progenitor of the Staffordshire Bull Terrier. A picture of the old English Bulldog from an ornament made in Britannia metal, probably late 18th Century, in the possession of James Crowe, Esq., Glasgow. Note the mutilation of the upper lips, done to effect the dog's easier breathing when at grips with an adversary!

3. 'Rosa', a 'Bull Terrier' bitch owned by the Baroness Burdett-Coutts. A painting by G. Morley, 1841. Note the similarity of type with present day specimens, apart from an obvious undershot jaw and rather feathery tail, indicative of Terrier influence.

4. Jim Simpson's (of Sydney) 'Billy'.

5. Mr. P. D. Perry's Ch. Bandits Brindamara.

Photo: C. M. Cooke & Son

6. Messrs. T. W. and J. Barnard's Ch. Chestonion Satan's Fireworks.

Photo: C: M. Cooke & Son

7. Mr. S. Davenport's 'Son of Roger'.

force and speed. As in other body departments dependent on activating muscle, bunchy muscles are inferior to the long well-toned variety which allow greater elasticity in movement. Stance is perfect only in an animal whose bones are correctly fashioned and are of the right length. Any mis-fit in the moulding of his parts will have its effect on the dog's conformation and staying power.

LOOK FOR: Good balance in the matter of height and breadth of hindquarters. Well developed second thighs are essential, as are hocks well let down. The limbs should be seen in parallel when the animal is moving away from you. Keep an eye open for the faults of 'cow-hocks' when the points of hocks turn inwards and 'in-toes' when the points of hocks turn outwards. Ensure good bend of stifle — this is very important. Any straightness in this area will limit the pushing and staying power of the dog and give a disagreeable prop-like effect to the hind limbs. This fault is often responsible for the slipping of the patella (kneecap), causing lameness because the limb is insufficiently bent and supported with muscle to hold it in place. Watch too for substantial muscle development in the inner and outer confines of the hindlegs and you should fault severely on degenerate posteriors.

Feet

The feet should be well padded, strong and of medium size.

The Staffordshire Bull Terrier has a muscular, supple paw. It should be well knit, but not a tight foot like that of the cat. It should be effective for instant and prolonged action. At the point of pasterns or wrists the feet turn out a little and although this formation militates a little against stylish forward stance in the show ring it was a necessary and useful feature in the fighting dog. Such a foot allowed considerable purchase of movement and maintained balance under stress. The approved shape can be likened to half hare, half cat foot, the toes well split up and with quite prominent knuckles. Thin, flat feet and feet with splayed toes are bad faults in an athletic breed.

FIG. 9.   FEET

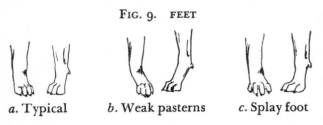

a. Typical   *b.* Weak pasterns   *c.* Splay foot

LOOK FOR: Well moulded feet in the desired form with an eye on the pasterns or wrists at which point any weakness in forelimb bone structure or development is likely to show.

Tail

The tail should be of medium length, low set, tapering to a point and carried rather low. It should not curl much and may be likened to an old-fashioned pump handle.

It is said the tail was a useful appendage to the fighting dog. He used it as a 'rudder' to twist and swivel himself round when the opportunity provided. The tail should not be too short as this detracts from the refinement of the show dog. It should not be too long as it lacks strength and spoils a dog's balance. A tail which measures to the point of hock

FIG. 10.   TAILS

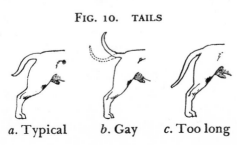

a. Typical   *b.* Gay   *c.* Too long

*Staffordshire bitch: Constones'
Owzat: owned by Mr. Snow*

Colour photos by Anne Cumbers

*Five-week-old puppies owned
by Mr. Taylor*

Staffordshire puppies owned by Mr. Frankhams

Staffordshire puppies owned by Mr. Taylor

Getting used to a collar at an early age

Good companions at a show

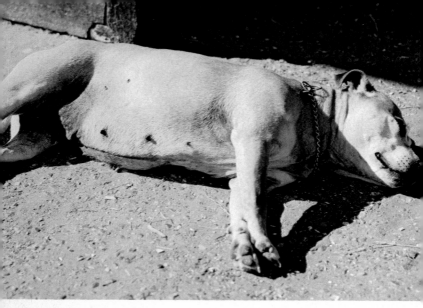

Staffordshire bitch enjoying the sun

Puppies in a good puppy box : owned by Mr. Frankham

is about right. Tail carriage depends largely upon the angle or position of the sacrum in relation to the spine. Where the sacrum finishes the root of the tail commences.

LOOK FOR: Typical pump handle tail of correct length with strong root. Fault gay tails or those that curl above the level of the back, particularly. A very low set tail is bad and occurs largely in dogs with a distinct falling-away at the croup, an unsightly weakness.

Coat

Smooth, short and close to the skin.

The Staffordshire Bull Terrier's coat is quite distinctive, best described as a medium coarse texture and pleasant to handle. It is very close fitting, but even on hard muscled dogs will tighten closer when the animal is fighting. When in this state it forms a leather-like armour protection to the body.

LOOK FOR: Quality in the coat texture and good condition. Fault long, coarse coats and any sign of ruff.

Colour

Red, fawn, white, black or blue, or any of these colours with white. Any shade of brindle or any shade of brindle with white. Black-and-tan and liver colour not to be encouraged.

You may prefer reds to brindles or vice versa. If you have such preference, forget it when you judge. Apart from the two un-favoured coat colourings, any colour is eligible for top honours. It is said that '. . . no good dog is a bad colour', and with reservation you can remember this when selecting your winners. Black-and-tan, which by the way, is a mixture of these colours distributed as on the Manchester Terrier, are not popular for if bred to the marking reproduces like germs in an epidemic. Livers too have a deleterious effect on the strain if allowed to breed.

LOOK FOR: Good, intense coat colours indicative of

sound pigmentation. Blacks are really brindles and even
on the blackest dog you will invariably find brindling
somewhere around the flank area. Examine the noses of
all exhibits, especially blues and fawns. The former appear
at times with slate blue noses, the latter, especially fallows,
with greyish noses. Both are faults. Check on eyes for faulty
pigmentation too. These should be dark, but you have the
word of the Standard to allow some relativity with coat
colour. Some blues and livers have gooseberry-like eyes
which are unpleasant and deserve penalising. Red-fawns
sometimes evince liver coloured eye-rims and around the
lips. Such specimens frequently have toenails of similar
hue. Truly a red dog is at his best with black nails and dark
points throughout. On white dogs or dogs with white
extending beyond the eye area you will only very occasionally find black eye rims, many such dogs being quite pink in
the region. Pink eye rims are stated faults, but when they
appear on dogs with white around the eye some elasticity
can be observed in judging the Staffordshire Bull Terrier.

Weight and Size

Weight: Dogs twenty-eight lb. to thirty-eight lb. Bitches,
twenty-four lb. to thirty-four lb. Height (at shoulder),
fourteen in. to sixteen in. these heights being related to
weights.

For a dog so modest in size as the Staffordshire this
section of the Standard appears one of quite wide extremes
in height and weight. It goes back to the early days when
there was considerable divergence in the size of specimens
available to support the breed at the first shows. It was
intended that none should feel ineligible to compete for
prizes so the Standard in this part was worded accordingly.
To-day, we try and produce a dog standing sixteen in. at
the shoulder and weighing thirty-eight lb. Provided such an
animal is well endowed with breed type and conforms to
the various sections of the Standard he is normally a well

balanced specimen. A bitch is allowed two in. less in height and four lb. in weight.

LOOK FOR: Good balance in the specimen before you. With a good specimen, one perhaps which is outstanding in the class before you, some deviation from the maximum weight may be permitted. Remember the Standard is intended as a guide. Slavish observance to any detailed measurements given will restrict your actions and interpretation of that Standard. Commonsense should prevail at all times when judging.

Faults

To be penalised in accordance with the severity of the fault: — light eyes or pink eye rims. Tail too long or badly curled. Non-conformation to the limits of height or weight. Full drop or prick ears. Undershot or overshot mouths. The following faults should debar a dog from winning any prize: Pink (Dudley) nose. Badly undershot or overshot mouth. Badly undershot — where the lower jaw protrudes to such an extent that the incisors of the upper jaw do not touch those of the lower jaw.

The more important faults have been discussed as their influence has affected the individual section of the Standard. This last part is self-explanatory, but possibly some further comment is warranted. The Dudley nose is entirely pinky-brown or flesh coloured and appears on certain fawns, reds and liver coloured brindles. It is a permanent fault and should not be confused with the Butterfly nose, commonly found on piebald dogs or those with considerable white markings around the muzzle area. Should this be seen in small puppies there is a fair chance that the nostrils will finish all black before dentition. However, if it is seen on an adult it is contrary to the black nose rule and is a fault therefore. The bright pink segments seen frequently on brindle muzzles and occasionally on reds in the proximity of the nostrils are not faults so long as the segments do not extend into the nostrils themselves. These should be black always.

Thus, you have been given the basic points of the breed Standard. Your final decision in judging should come when you have completed an evaluation of the individual points and combined the findings. Although it has been pointed out to the judge that there are faults and he must be aware of these in judging, it is not suggested that he should approach his task in a negative manner such as judging freedom from faults would suggest. All judging should be done positively on the good points of the exhibit. If you judge on faults and base your judgment on faults you do no more for the breed than to lower the average level of that breed to sound but type-less individuals. Neither should judging be confined to solitary points of excellence, like good heads, forgetting meanwhile the rest of the animal with qualities of temperament and body balance overlooked. Several once-respected breeds have for this reason fallen by the wayside and it is not intended that the Staffordshire Bull Terrier should do likewise.

CHAPTER FOUR

Buying Your Puppy

YOU MAY have bought this little book after the purchase of your puppy with a view to learning more about the breed. On the other hand, you may be one who prefers to read and learn before purchasing. Into whichever category you fall I hope the contents of these pages prove useful to you. Small puppies are chancey things to buy if you have exhibiting in mind. If you want a pet perhaps the finer points are not of paramount importance. Nevertheless, remember that a typical specimen of the breed need cost little more than an ordinary one. If you own a pedigree dog of a certain breed you want to have it recognised for what it is when you are out and more important to everyone − you buy a certain breed for its character. This character with correct breed temperament are vital ingredients. A Staffordshire Bull Terrier is purchased by the man or woman who wants an 'honest' dog − a dog to guard, to be fearless, to use his brains, to be clean in his ways and to be reliable with children. The true Stafford conforms thus. A well bred one carries these characteristics but an ill-bred one, as with dogs of any breed, can fail in some or all respects.

If you want a Stafford of correct character but not necessarily with finer show points you can buy one and in such purchase go to a reliable breeder who will advise you and charge you accordingly. However, if you want a superior specimen with exhibiting in mind then it is better to delay your purchase until you have the opportunity of buying a puppy of perhaps four to six months of age.

Younger ones often look good but change alarmingly in the process of growing so that the cobby, solid little dog of two months looks like a Whippet at four months! At the more advanced ages you should be able to see more or less what you are investing in. At least, your chances of procuring a show specimen are proportionately higher. Take your time about such a purchase — you will find that patience will pay dividends. The opportunities of buying puppies of an age of four to six months are seldom frequent. Most breeders have their puppies off their hands by the time they are two months old. Some breeders 'run on' a show prospect for their own consideration, then if the animal does not come up to their hopes they offer it for sale. You should always check the validity of the reasons given you for the sale of older puppies. If you feel doubtful as to your own ability to decide then take along an informed friend or perhaps a qualified person who will help you for a small fee. One of the first things you should look at in an older puppy offered for sale apart from its soundness is its mouth. So many breeders run on show prospects — marvellous specimens in many respects, but which are giving indications of going undershot. This means the lower jaw is beginning to project beyond the upper one (Bulldog-fashion). Refer to the chapter on the Standard and my sketches to illustrate this feature.

Many good puppies never see the show ring because of this fault and many puppies never give an indication of this propensity until they have lost their milk teeth, so you need to make sure for your own good that you are not buying a dog with such a fault or one which may well have the fault later with complete dentition. It is probable that you will wish to buy a bitch. Frankly, this is the wiser course. A bitch, if she does not come up to your expectations in show ring potential can always be the medium which will allow you to breed and probably produce for you the show dog that you want. A well-bred bitch puppy is an asset, of that you need have no doubts. When you have the opportunity to buy one take your time in assessing her. If she is to be a good whelper she should have a wide pelvis. If you are unsure of what this means get your veterinary surgeon's approval before you confirm purchase. Some strains, owing to their having been bred by faddists who concentrated on marvellous heads and fronts, have hind-quarters which in the process have been overlooked. Consequently, the hindquarters in such stock have become degenerate, the pelvic structure tightened to a point which would make whelping in some individuals extremely difficult. Any breeder or vendor selling a puppy rather older than the usual going-away time of two to three months should have no objection to your having the animal on at least seven days approval or for you to obtain veterinary confirmation that your new purchase is a sound one. Naturally, such professional services entail fees which would in such instances be your own responsibility.

Check with the owner of the puppy for any unpleasant tendencies – you will soon find these out for yourself anyway if any exist. However, forewarned is forearmed, as they say, and you can start at once to rectify doubtful features in a youngster's initial training. In effect, you will have to ensure that your puppy is as free from faults in her make, type and temperament, as possible. The pedigree should be studied too. If you have never handled such a document before and feel unable to interpret it, seek the opinion of a competent person. You will then avoid the purchase of a puppy which is closely in-bred. Puppies so bred may appear quite useful in the early stages, but the system will just as easily heighten unfavourable charac-teristics as it will 'fix' good ones. Always try and see the parents of the puppy you purchase. Such forebears or those immediate to the parents should not have bad mouths, lack pigmentation or have Dudley (brown) noses for these are transmittable faults. If you are buying a bitch puppy find out how her dam behaved as a mother. A bad dam, unable to rear puppies and unreliable with the whelps is a serious worry and expense, quite apart from the fact that frequently the female offspring inherit the characteristic! Avoid small bitches — these seldom make satisfactory and easy whelpers, neither are they popular as show winners.

When you pick up your puppy you should feel substance — not just skin and bone! Stand the puppy up on the table just as though you were placing her there to be judged. She will wriggle and complain, but you should be able to get a good clear profile view of her. She should be 'chunky' — plenty of head and ample depth of skull — a muzzle which at this stage should appear rather *too* short. Wrinkling of the skin over the skull and in the head area generally is a fair sign that room is there for substantial filling out. Neck, shoulders, forequarters, ribs should feel bulky and well knit together when you put your two hands over the top of the withers. Bone should be ample rather than big — too much bone indicates a coarse one. Feet should be neat rather than big. Put your hand clear between the front legs flat on to the brisket and the chest. Feel the 'room' which exists between the forelegs where they join the body. Move your hand around and seek for width which will allow development, but remember the forelegs and elbow area should be firm — not tight, but firm. A wide chest between loose forequarters is no advantage. So often you will get elbows which point outwards instead of lying firmly in line with the front legs. These represent a fault which any judge will see in the ring and which is a structural weakness.

If, when stood up and looked at in profile your puppy stands in an imaginary square, then she may well promise well in conformation. Look at her mouth. If she already shows signs of an undershot jaw then reject her for the odds against correction are too great. The upper teeth should quite obviously rest over and on to the lower teeth.

Should you be buying a male, check the genitals. Both testicles should be visible or there to the touch in an animal of four months or over. Sometimes in dogs of six or seven weeks of age they can be seen, but in young puppies indetermination of this matter after examination is not conclusive. A small umbilical hernia (bump on navel) on either dog or bitch puppy need not put you off a specimen which satisfies you completely in all other respects. Such a protuberance will cause no inconvenience to the animal and if required can be dealt with by your veterinary surgeon quite quickly and simply.

CHAPTER FIVE

Feeding and General Care

YOU ARE now the proud owner of a Staffordshire Bull Terrier. No doubt you have high hopes of his future as a show winner but whether you have ambitions in this direction or not you will want a nice looking typical specimen with whom you can look forward to many years of enjoyable companionship.

Good feeding and regular meal times are of paramount importance in achieving good results with dogs. Well balanced health-giving meals produce bright eyes, glossy coats and active animals with happy dispositions. If you keep a dog it is up to you to see he is fed and cared for properly. Your interest in this is apparent or you would not be reading this little book.

Remember with a small puppy 'little and often' is the rule in feeding. We will assume he is at a stage, say around the eight weeks mark, when he requires four meals a day, split up at four-hourly intervals. The purpose of this division of the bulk feeding is to ensure the puppy is not given too much at any one meal. This would cause distension in an eager feeder with the resulting digestive troubles. Feeding should be in accordance with your domestic convenience and can be adapted to your own methods, but the following menu will serve as a useful guide:

8 a.m.   Milky meal. The milk should be at blood heat and can be served on cereal — 'Weetabix' and similar. The baby food 'Farex' is excellent and so is light porridge.

12 noon   Meat meal. Good quality lean meat — shin of

beef, chopped small or shredded, but not minced as this does not allow the stomach juices full play. Make some warm gravy with 'Oxo' or similar and pour it over the meat which has been mixed with biscuit meal such as 'Saval' or rusks (bread baked in the oven). Boiled vegetable liquid can replace the gravy at times. Never feed vegetables themselves to a puppy under six months of age.

4.30 p.m. Warm milk or gravy over rusks.

8 p.m. Repeat as for the noon meal.

If the puppy is moving about late at night owing to your tardy retirement he can be given a saucer of warm milk as a nightcap.

Vitamin additives are useful in growing puppies. Vitamin A which is essential for growth can be found in the juice obtained from boiled endives, carrot and turnip top. Vitamin D is for bone development and all foods strong in calcium and phosphorus apply here. You can get powdered calcium from your chemist and sprinkle a little of this (say as much as will cover a sixpenny piece) over your puppy's evening meal. He should have coarse cod-liver oil occasionally – perhaps four times a week during winter months, but use olive oil in similar measure during the summer months.

Feeding up to maturity

By the time your puppy has entered into the next stage and reached the age of four months he will have reduced his number of daily meals to three. Dogs often do this themselves by ignoring one meal at this stage. It is usually either the breakfast meal or the tea meal. If you find this happens heed the suggestion and begin to step up the amounts of the other remaining meals. Make sure, however, that his stomach does not distend after eating as this will indicate he is having too much at a 'sitting'. A good pointer as to quantity is to watch a dog eat — when he stops for his first breath then that is where you want to remove the plate!

Keep up the standard and quality of the food until the age of six or seven months when he can begin to feed like an adult. Two meals a day should be adequate for this — a light one of a little meat and a few biscuits at mid-day and the main meal, almost entirely of raw lean meat, in the evening. An adult Staffordshire should be fed dry — sloppy food is useless to the older dog. He is best fed after his evening exercise so that he can relax and get the most nutritive effect from his meal. Water should be down at all times and it should be changed at frequent intervals during the day. White fish, carefully steamed and boned, is an alternative you can use to advantage.

Do not let him come into contact with rabbit or poultry bones as these are dangerous. However, if he eats such animals on killing them as a wild dog might, there is no harm in them. The best bone for a Stafford, if he must have one, is the big knuckle or marrow bone which he cannot so easily crush between his jaws. However, if you feel that your dog has a tendency towards the undershot mouth best keep bones away entirely for they will do little other than to promote the fault.

The average grown dog of this breed needs at least one lb. raw, fresh meat daily. If you cannot manage this, then certainly no less than half a lb. and make up the volume with some other form of food. If you want a good-looking, healthy dog with bright eyes, glossy coat and ample vigour do not attempt any economies in feeding, for good food and attention are an insurance.

Inoculation

The virus diseases which commonly beset the dog are Distemper, Hard Pad and Hepatitis, although the incidence of all these have been lessened considerably by the progress of modern veterinary medicine. A well-known immuniser such as 'Epivax-Plus' which effectively copes with all three viruses is marketed by Burroughes Wellcome and is competent to give life-long protection to your dog against these scourges which in the old days wiped out entire kennels.

The time for having your puppy inoculated should be determined by your vet. Tell him how old your dog is in weeks and he will tell you when he wants to effect the immunisation. It is a good thing to have done. Staffordshire Bull Terriers are hardy creatures but they are liable to pick up anything although perhaps not to the extent of some other breeds.

Before and even after your puppy has been inoculated you should take pains to ensure it does not come into dangerous contact with places where these diseases and others might lurk. Lamp-posts, street corners and stray dogs being three examples.

Guard too against Leptospirosis, a dread disease to dogs and one carried by rats. Consult your vet about this and have your puppy immunised against this one too.

Elementary obedience training

Perhaps an apt heading for this section would be 'Manners Maketh Dog'. There is little doubt that to enjoy the companionship of a dog to the full, his good behaviour in the home and in public is essential. When you first acquire your puppy and see it running around the home, playful but easy enough to direct, no doubt you will have visions of it as a tractable companion, obedient to the word of command and in fact, a 'gem' of a dog. If you want results like this then it is up to you. As with children, obedience is never achieved without firm and tolerant handling. You need, as well, patience and consistency. Never try and teach a puppy anything if your nerves are frayed for by so doing you will undo all that you have previously achieved.

The initial training which must be applied to your puppy is to make him house clean. The instant he awakens from a sleep or immediately following upon his meals he should be put outside with the command 'Up the garden'. Wait until he has done what he went out for and then praise him. During the initial period he will make a few mistakes — all puppies do. Show him the offending spot and scold him. Say 'Bad dog' and put him outside and close the door on him. It may well be several weeks before he is reliably clean at night, but with such training his cleanliness during the daytime should be assured. Try and be around during the critical times when he might wish to go outside within the first two or three weeks of training and do not blame him if he makes a mistake when you are not present to help him in the training.

The first real lesson and to my mind, a most important one, is to teach your puppy to come to hand immediately upon call. Nothing is more infuriating and humiliating than to try and catch a deliberately elusive puppy in an open space such as a park. Anyone who has fumed and perspired at this task will appreciate my point.

Never chase a puppy in an effort to catch him. The average pup interprets this as a great game and enters into it to the full, quite overlooking your frustration and annoyance. Have in your hand a small titbit and call the puppy with his name and the command 'Come!' You may have to wait sometime for a positive response but keep calling in a pleasant tone of voice and when he does obey give him the titbit, tell him what a good dog he has been and make a fuss of him. A few repetitions of this exercise and he will quickly learn that he gets a pleasant reward when he comes to you. Before you let your puppy loose out of doors be sure you have trained to obey this command. It is advisable not to make a practice of always putting him back on his leash when he has been called to you. He could associate the idea of being called as an end to his enjoyed freedom and that might set him back a little in his training.

A dog which walks on the leash without pulling your arm out of its socket is a pleasure to take out. Staffordshire Bull Terrier youngsters are inclined to pull and you should start training them early in life. Start your puppy on a collar and lead in the garden or somewhere unrestricted where he is unlikely to get caught up in all sorts of obstacles. He will probably take an instant dislike to it, pulling in all directions in an effort to get loose. Stand your ground, keep hold of the lead and let him find out for himself how unpleasant it is to fight against that thing around his neck. Eventually, he will quieten and you can pat him to give him confidence. Then try walking a few steps. He will now shoot either forwards or backwards. If backwards, give a slight jerk on the lead, encouraging him in the right direction. If forward, jerk the lead to stop him. He will speedily find it infinitely more comfortable to walk on a loose lead. You may find that he is one of those who lays flat on the ground with an expression which says 'I won't!'. If so, you can try encouraging him with a titbit, but if this fails you must be firm and drag him along a short way when he will most certainly get up, for the friction on his feet will be found most unpleasant. Praise him now and remember that dogs generally like to please their owners so always give plenty of praise when he has done what you have asked of him.

To have a dog which will stay in a given place for any length of time is very valuable. The most comfortable position for a dog to maintain is the down position. Put your dog down, stand just in front of him with the command 'Stay!' — then move back a step. If he moves, again put him down and repeat the command. After a few tries you will find he will stay and now praise him. You can now begin lengthening the distance between you by moving gradually further and further back until he will stay with a considerable distance between you. The amount of time taken from the time you leave him to your return can be varied, but always come back and praise him when he has done well. This exercise can be extended so that you can go completely out of his sight for varying intervals.

Perhaps the most annoying habit a dog can have is jumping up at everyone in sight. This may be a nice way of greeting when you return home after an absence but it is not to be encouraged if the dog has muddy paws and the recipient of his affections has on a light coloured coat! Discourage the puppy strongly in this habit — give the firm command 'Off!' and push him away. If he persists give him a sharp slap across the front legs with a rolled-up newspaper which makes a loud noise but does no harm physically.

Never let your puppy cultivate habits, which while amusing enough when the animal is in puppyhood become embarrassments in a powerful adult. Do not allow a puppy or dog to be teased for this causes bad temper in an animal, more than any other reason. Remember that you want your adult dog to be a reliable and pleasant companion who will always do you credit wherever you may take him. Treat him sensibly therefore and with kindness too. He will more than re-pay you with his unquestioning loyalty for the time you have spent on teaching him his manners.

Car travel

Many dogs suffer miserably travelling in the back seat of a motor car or in fact on any journey, even by 'bus or train'. It is best never to feed a dog at least three or four hours before taking him on a long trip. This will minimise the risk of sickness. Many dogs are sick in the car solely for psychological reasons. As young puppies they were fed before being taken out and they were sick. This might have happened once or twice and from that time onwards the trip in the car was associated with a nausea and sure enough vomiting would take place, even if the dog had nothing in his stomach. If you have such a dog he can be broken of this unfortunate malady by taking him on short trips in the car — the first time perhaps for a trip around the block, the next time twice around the block, the third time a mile, then two miles and so on, without giving him time to be sick! Once he gets used to his car trip without the expected sickness he will be cured.

Fighting

Sooner or later in a dog's life, regardless of his breed, he will get into a scrap. Most breeds indulge themselves for a moment or two then break it up and retire victor or vanquished, as the case may be. Not so the Staffordshire Bull Terrier who was never made to retire gracefully and although he may not enter a fight without provocation, if he is forced into it he may well finish it! This means that you should have him trained either to be called off when a fight looks imminent or at least to respond, if unwillingly, to your efforts in taking him off his adversary. The method of separating a pair of fighting dogs is not a simple one when a Staffordshire Bull Terrier is involved, for one in combat fills out his close-fitting coat even more, making it into what is virtually a suit of armour. This means that not only is it difficult for his enemy to get a mouthful of flesh, but for you to take hold of him. Ensure therefore, that he wears a strong strap leather collar at all times (you can always dress him in a handsome studded one on special occasions), so that he can be grabbed if necessary.

Should he become embroiled in a fight and you have proved unsuccessful in calling him off, try and confine the fighting pair to a corner or somewhere to prevent it becoming a running battle in which any efforts to separate would be frustrated. Two people are better than one in coping with a dog-fight and you should endeavour to enlist the aid of the other owner. He should hold his dog steady as it will almost certainly be your dog which has secured the first hold. You should stand astride the loins of your dog and grip him firmly with your knees to immobilise his hind-quarters which he will be using to improve his position in the fight. Bring your hand round and under his collar, take it and twist it as strongly as you can, bringing considerable pressure to bear on your dog's windpipe. Do *not* drag your dog away at this stage, rather press his nose into the other dog. This, together with the effect of the ever-tightening collar will cause him eventually, to take breath. At this point then, you draw him away and remove him at once from the scene, making sure the other dog's owner is instructed to hold on to his charge meanwhile. Take care at all times that your hands are kept beyond the range of both mouths during the incident!

From the foregoing section some people may well think a Staffordshire Bull Terrier could prove an embarrassment. This is not so, for the average dog of this breed is a good honest animal. He will not attack unless he is sorely provoked and I am certain you do not want a dog which will run away from or ignore indefinitely the insults of others. He knows how to select friend from foe and treats each with the affection or firmness it warrants. As a guard for property or the protection of his master or mistress he excels — in fact he seldom has to do much apart from look at any intending attacker for his appearance is formidable to the wrong-doer. With small children he is superb — it is doubtful if another breed exists which can equal him, apart from the Bulldog, perhaps, from whom he has inherited this great characteristic. Indignities, minor cruelties, which so many children perpetrate on their dogs out of the sight of their parents, are suffered gladly. In fact, I am not at all sure at times whether these dogs do not enjoy such things! Certainly, they tolerate them and with never a murmur or even the slightest warning.

Exercise

The Staffordshire Bull Terrier is a highly adaptable dog. He thrives well on the farm, in a city flat or in a kennel. Abroad he does well in the stickiest climate or in the snow. He will take as much exercise as you can give him or as little as you find convenient by circumstances. Naturally, it is better if you can give part of your day to his walk and make a regular feature of it for by doing so you will keep him fit and see the benefit of the exercise in his sparkling eyes and glistening coat. The best exercise for a Stafford is on hard ground and on the lead. The lead ensures a steady, determined motion, better for muscle development and the hard ground keeps his feet closely knit and his pasterns strong, as well as develop the quarters. Extra to the steady walk which can extend to as many miles as you can tackle yourself, he can be allowed loose for a period of free movement. When you do this, make sure it is in a park or open space away from the dangers of traffic. Impulsiveness in the breed makes them see little danger in cars and transport — many of these dogs get run over every year solely for this reason, not from the usual reason which is carelessness. If you find a hill or a steep bank good development of the hindquarters can be encouraged by throwing a ball up the slope for the dog to retrieve. Do this regularly and you will soon notice a great improvement. Give the dog an old motor cycle tyre to drag around and you will quickly notice how great become his jaw muscles. Leave him with a weighty log which he can just lift and what an iron-muscled neck he will get! Do not allow him to get fat, for no Bull Terrier should carry fat other than what gives him a pleasing line for the show ring. The old fighting dogs were bereft of it — in fact some of the forty lb. dogs you see in the show ring to-day could be brought down to around

thirty lb. in fighting condition and in those days they knew
how to exercise them!

Kennelling

I am no great believer in kennelled dogs. Of course, if
you keep a lot you have to keep them in this way, but
a kennel means solitary confinement to a dog and I think
this means mental suffering and considerable loss in intelligence. If you have several dogs and cannot possibly
accommodate them in the home at least give them turns
to see the fireside. Unfortunately, a dog which has seen
'the other side of the fence' wants it all the time — this is
natural. However, animals become trained to routine and it
should be within the powers of any intelligent kennel owner
to organise something of this kind for the welfare of his
dogs.

The Staffordshire is ideal when he is made a member of
the family circle. Dogs kept indoors make better guards
anyway — they get to know the home, get to love it and
people in it. What they know and love they want to
protect. A kennel dog may warn with his barking, but he is
not much good at the end of the garden behind a locked
door. The indoors dog is on the spot. He can cope with an
intruder — in fact, not many intruders are brave enough
when they know they have to face a Staffordshire Bull
Terrier. I have supplied many public houses with dogs of
this breed — many of these establishments having had
burglars at regular intervals. Once the dog is installed and
allowed to show himself inside the bar at closing time they
just do not come any more! So keep your dog indoors if
you can. If you cannot, then ensure comfortable, warm and
draught-free quarters outside. Find a suitable spot first, one
which is not overshadowed with foliage and where the
sunlight and fresh air can reach. The kennel itself should
face south or south-west and be built over well drained
ground away from the wind.

You can buy some excellent pre-fabricated kennels. There are a number on the market and best place to inspect the variety available is at one of the big Agricultural shows which are held in the summer — Handsworth Park, Birmingham and Abbey Park, Leicester are two which spring to mind. If you envisage starting a small breeding kennel you may consider a range of four compartments, but ensure you have an isolated one as well in case you have a sick animal at some time. For the Staffordshire Bull Terrier, an ideal floor space is twenty-five sq. ft. certainly not less than sixteen sq. ft. per dog with an adequate run of between six to nine ft. The run should be surrounded by strong chain-link fencing which can well be ten ft. high as the Staffordshire Bull Terrier is quite an athletic dog and can reach considerable heights even from a standing jump. If the fence has to be lower than that try and arrange a wire-netting roof. The height inside the kennels should be at least six ft. to allow comfortable entry and for you to stand inside. Nothing is more irritating than to have to work bent up like a hairpin.

The dogs' sleeping benches must be raised from the kennel floor. Draughts kill dogs and this is important. The benches should slide out or be detachable in some way and the general style of the kennel should be such that scrupulous hygeine can be observed. Cleanliness in a kennel is a primary consideration. Disinfection and clean straw or bedding should be attended to daily and fresh clean water should be supplied twice a day.

Grooming

There is little to do in this respect. The average Stafford shire Bull Terrier, even he with a great deal of white in his coat usually looks spotless. It is a very clean breed, physically and mentally, but obviously an owner should give his dog daily attention and this with a hound-glove or semi-harsh brush, polishing over with a soft dry chamois leather. However, good coats come mainly from good feeding, and this is the primary consideration.

Do not bathe your dog too often. Once a year is usually enough for the house-dog, although a kennel dog sleeping on straw may need more regular attention. Of course, if the dog rolls in some foreign matter he will need a bath but remember that baths should be given on warm days or in a place free from draughts. A thorough drying down should be given, especially underneath the dog and around the genitals. Never bathe small puppies. Little ones like this may well be put back by such treatment.

Games

The Staffordshire Bull Terrier likes a good game. In fact he will enter into the spirit of one with such zest at times, that you might wish you had never started it! This is a very athletic breed and a sound, healthy dog can perform great feats of jumping and considerable turns of speed. Such an animal can keep up with a Whippet for the first eighty yards of the chase and this is remarkable in such a powerful solid dog. One can get over a ten ft. fence, mainly by jumping, the rest of the way scrambling over the obstacle. A ball thrown into the air will be trapped neatly without the slightest bounce when it reaches the ground or caught mid-air in a cavernous mouth. Throw no sticks, however, when two or more dogs are loose together. The one who grabs the stick first will shake it and twist it in his pleasure and the ends constitute a danger to his companions' eyes. Quite apart from this, stick games seem to start quarrels and are best left alone with other than the solitary dog to enjoy them.

Keep an eye on the progress of the game. It is best to make games short and sweet, for dogs highly trained in physical prowess are apt to become elated quickly and the Stafford-shire is no exception. Such a state is indicated by the eyes which tend to glaze over a little. Once you see this stop the game for the dog himself will never know when to stop.

When you leave dogs at home separate them. Never have two together unattended. If the delay before your return is too long they may well start a game of their own — a little all-in wrestling or ear chewing and such pastimes sometimes go wrong and tempers become frayed. A fight once started and which develops without interference can end in the death of one or both the combatants. I could give a number of examples, two from personal experience. Care in segregating individuals to different rooms before you go out is essential and can save you a lot of money and heartache.

CHAPTER SIX

Ailments

FORTUNATELY, few ailments beset a healthy Staffordshire Bull Terrier. The breed is very hardy and strongly constituted and one which is well fed and maintained and has had his inoculations seldom suffers the many different sicknesses which seem to attack some breeds. I have selected a few ailments, such as might be encountered by the average owner. These I have dealt with briefly, but at sufficient length to give at least some idea of the symptoms and how to proceed before enlisting the aid of your veterinary surgeon. The more serious virus diseases such as Distemper, Hard-Pad, Hepatitis and Leptospirosis can be guarded against by inoculation. It is the duty of every dog owner to take such precautions, as immunization is effective for a lifetime.

ABNORMALITIES. The common abnormalities found at birth are Cleft Palate, Hare Lip and Screw Tail. The first two are not uncommon malformations and can be detected in a new-born puppy by the way it holds open its mouth. Such puppies are unable to feed from their dam and usually fade and die. It is better to put them down at once. The screw tail, reminiscent of the Bulldog's tail is an inheritance from that breed. A puppy with this defect is fit only as a pet and would have no worth in the show ring.

ANAL GLANDS. These glands are situated on either side of the anus, and with correct feeding and normal motions they give little trouble. However, at times they become clogged and often infected, causing the animal no little discomfort. The dog so affected will drag his rear end along the ground and give every indication of the irritation. To treat, stand the dog on a table at manageable level. Take a fair-sized pad of cotton wool in one hand and raise the dog's tail with the other. Place the pad firmly over the glands and press, squeezing inwards and upwards. The offending matter will be expelled from the glands and your dog will regain his comfort. If the condition is one of long-standing keep an eye open for abscesses and if any are indicated consult your veterinary surgeon.

CONSTIPATION. The symptoms are obvious and the treatment simple. Faulty diet is the main cause of this complaint and green vegetables should be introduced to the feed at once. Often, too much biscuit meal and insufficient meat and vegetable juices is the cause, the motions being hard and pale in colour. If the condition persists a tea-spoonful of liquid paraffin will prove effective as a laxative or a good proprietary medicine can be administered to advantage.

CYSTS. Your first indication of these may be when you see the dog continually licking between his toes and pads. Cysts may occur over the body area too and quite apart from their unsightliness they cause the dog considerable discomfort. Some veterinary surgeons will cut them out, but the main cause is faulty diet and it is better to remove the cause of the cysts. I have seen a fully grown dog very distressed with inter-digital cysts. The animal was fed entirely on fresh raw meat. This was changed to a well-known brand of tinned meat. Almost at once the condition disappeared. Three months later when raw meat was re-introduced the cysts returned but went again as soon as the tinned food was substituted. In such matters experimentation plays a large part, but in all cases where cysts are in evidence your first attempt to cure must be with the dog's diet.

Another form of cyst commonly occurs in mid-summer, when grass spears and the awns of wild meadow barley enter the soft skin between the dog's toes. Particles of flint from newly tarred roads may be responsible too. In such cases remove the offending object with tweezers and bathe the parts with a warm boracic solution or similar. Gravel or road tar adhering to the pads can be removed by holding the dog's foot in a bowl of turpentine or methylated spirit. Make sure afterwards that no trace of these spirits remain for the animal to lick.

DEW CLAWS. All puppies have these rudimentary digits on the fore-legs, some on the hind-legs. The latter must be removed as soon as the puppies are four days old. The dew-claws on the front legs can be removed or allowed to remain according to the breeder's discretion. Many Staffordshire Bull Terrier people like to see them on and I have never found a dog suffer any disadvantages by having them. It is normal to get your veterinary surgeon to remove them, but if you are competent to do the job yourself use a pair of sterilized snub-nosed scissors, cutting as near to the limb as possible. Superfluous bleeding can be stemmed with Friars Balsam and as with any minor operation of this kind a close watch should be kept on the wounds until they have healed.

DIARRHOEA. When you see a dog with this you should treat the matter seriously and make immediate efforts to bind the motions. Take the animal off meat at once, confining his feed to milky meals possibly with some arrowroot added. The dog can return to meat meals within two or three days when the condition has been corrected.

*DISTEMPER. This disease, seldom heard of to-day, due to the success of modern veterinary science is usually indicated by loss of appetite, husky cough, extreme lassitude, discharges from eyes and nose and bowel upset

* Dogs diagnosed as suffering from these diseases should be isolated at once.

with consequent rise in temperature. Let your vet take charge immediately.

EARS. Rough-edged ears are a nuisance and unsightly. When neglected the outer edges become serrated and unpleasantly dry to touch. A good remedy is 'Vaseline' Hair Tonic or a little 'Silvikrin' worked into the affected area, left to dry then shampoo-ed off. Treated twice a week for a month a cure should be effected, but take care the inner ear is protected during application.

EYES. If your dog has running, watery eyes and this symptom is not associated with others which might indicate something more serious, it is probably a case of simple Conjunctivitis, a condition which can prove stubborn, or at least recurring. Wipe the eyes clean, then insert a globule of 'Golden Eye Ointment' or its veterinary equivalent.

The same ointment may be applied to the inner surface of the lower lids of the eyes to ease soreness which will be experienced when your dog has inverted eyelashes, a not uncommon complaint in the breed. Irritation of the eyeballs is experienced and it is wise to enlist the aid of your veterinary surgeon as a minor operation can effect a permanent cure.

*HARD PAD. This is really canine Encephalitis and is quite serious. The symptoms are not dissimilar to those of Distemper. Occasionally, the pads of the feet and the nostrils will harden and thicken, with some evidence of paralysis in parts. This is one for your vet, but note that after-care and nursing plays an important part in the patient's speedy recovery.

*HEPATITIS. The symptoms are again very similar to those of Distemper and can often be confused with that disease. Early action is essential and your vet should be called in at once.

* Dogs diagnosed as suffering from these diseases should be isolated at once.

LEPTOSPIROSIS. A disease which is becoming commoner. You should avail yourself of the inoculation which is an effective guard. The virus is carried by rats and a dog can become infected by being bitten by one or coming into contact with food which has been fouled by rats. Symptoms of the disease are fever, vomiting, diarrhoea, lassitude and some bleeding of the gums. Call in your vet immediately and it would be wise to take steps to dispose of any rats about the place.

MANGE. *Sarcoptic.* (Synonymous with Scabies in humans) A cure can be effected on this form which is evidenced by small bare patches appearing initially on the head and ears. The underparts, i.e. the belly and groin areas often swell and redden and the dog will lacerate himself in his irritation. Proprietary mange cures can be used to good effect and the dog bathed in one three times a week.

Follicular. Very little is known about this form and it is often fatal. The bare, slate blue patches often become pustular and emit a foul smell. Benzyl benzoate emulsion or similar agent can be applied and in cases where the condition has been caught early, this can have good effect, in conjunction with warm peroxide of hydrogen solution used for local bathing.

In the event of either conditions the affected animal should be isolated and his bedding burnt at once, his kennel disinfected also his personal equipment.

Apart from the two foregoing kinds of mange to which the Staffordshire can become a victim, there is another skin trouble to which he is comparatively prone and far more likely to have than these. This trouble he would have appeared to inherit from his ancestor the Bulldog. Signs of bareness in patches on the coat become evident mainly during his teething period or at times in later life when his resistance is lower than normal, for example after a protracted illness. These small patches which are usually seen on the cheeks, head and shoulders, gradually increase in size. The dog seldom gives any indication of discomfort, but should the marks become pustular the dog may scratch. The symptoms are almost identical with those of Follicular Mange and this scourge is frequently diagnosed by veterinary surgeons who have taken scrapings from the affected parts. For this reason whole litters have been put down by breeders who could not face the virtually hopeless task of the cure, for that disease is progressive and highly unsatisfactory to treat. I have often thought that less is known in medical circles about human and canine dermatology than authorities care to admit. The skin trouble so common to our breed need cause no fears for although I believe it akin to the deadly follicular variety it is a comparatively harmless form. It is in fact 'the old Bulldog baldness' and is no more than a simple thyroid deficiency which can be rectified or ignored, according to your fancy. Those owners who are worried by it should discuss the matter with their vets and endeavour to get professional blessing to treatment of this cause. I have cured a four month old Staffordshire puppy, almost bereft of coat. He was given one-grain veterinary Thyroid Glandular tablets over a three week period. The dosage was two a day for the first week, followed by one a day for the following two weeks. The treatment was not extended beyond this period as the dog's coat was already growing in profusion. Remember however, that your vet will have first hand knowledge of your particular case and you should never take treatment into your own hands without prior reference to him.

The type of mange we have discussed does not appear contagious and although many people apply external lotions to prevent undue spread of the bareness, these emulsions appear to have little effect, for it is within the dog that treatment is necessary. Firstly, remove all excess fat from the dog's body, bringing him to a high degree of fitness. Ensure he is free from worms and that his bowels are thoroughly cleansed. A small teaspoonful of bicarbonate of soda should be added to a light morning meal daily.

The bare patches appear at any stage in the teething period which can extend from approximately three to seven months. Skin trouble appearing on a puppy of say, four months may last proportionately longer than on one which shows no signs of it until he is six months old, for complete dentition (i.e. when the dog has his permanent teeth) is the stage at which you can reasonably expect the condition to disappear. It is not unlike teething rash in a baby — like that eruption it goes when the baby has its teeth through and body resistance has returned to normal. Inherited weaknesses, and in my opinion this skin trouble is an example, are often latent while the animal is healthy, but let that fitness stray below par and it will come to the surface.

It does not follow that your Staffordshire will have these patches. Many go through life without any deterioration of coat. In fact, recent years have shown some lessening in the number of cases. I have had a number of puppies which suffered the occasional bare patch, but apart from the four month old one referred to above, and this was in 1947, I have ignored them, knowing full well the condition would mend in its own time, which it did, without treatment.

MONORCHIDISM and CRYPTORCHIDISM. These malformations apply only to the male dog, of course. A monorchid is one in which only one testicle has descended into the scrotum. Such an animal may have been born with only one, but many have the second testicle retained in the abdomen. A cryptorchid is a dog with neither testicle descended into the scrotum. He may have none or both may be retained in his abdomen. The condition is stated to be hereditary, but correction has been effected in some instances by judicious hormone injections. Some breeders

8. Mr. T. Field's Ch. Bandits Brintiga.

9. An attractive litter by N.Z. Ch. Weycombe Timothy. *By courtesy of Mrs. Marion Forester.*

10. Mr. M. Tranter's Ch. Bandits Red Armour.

11. Messrs. Holden and Potter's 'Sans Cooper'.

12. Mr. Alan Meredith with his late Ch. Fancy Fay of Summermuir.

13. Mr. W. Cutler's Ch. Gentleman Bruce earning money for Charity at Portsmouth and Southsea Open Show, 1960.

Photo: Portsmouth & Sunderland Newspapers Ltd.

consider it unwise to include a dog so afflicted in their breeding programmes, for if indeed it is hereditary the malformation can be passed on to future generations. This would seem to be the official viewpoint too, for as from 1st January, 1959, The Kennel Club disqualified all such dogs from the show ring. Likewise, a decree was passed that any male dog to be exported abroad should be examined by a qualified person to determine his entirety and a document signed to confirm this state.

POISONING. It is to be hoped that you will have no need for this section, but if so, the following emergency instructions should prove useful. Firstly give the dog an immediate emetic. The most effective are (i) a dessert-spoonful of salt in a half tumbler of water, (ii) a similar solution of mustard, (iii) a marble sized lump of common soda. Telephone your vet immediately and describe the symptoms of the poisoning and treat according to his advice. If the dog has vomited the contents of his stomach you can give him whites of eggs in milk.

UMBILICAL HERNIA. This is a swelling or bump on the dog's navel. It is not uncommon on a puppy which is the first-born from an inexperienced bitch, whelping for the first time. The dam, often worried and bemused by the situation may be careless in nipping off the umbilical cord, dragging at it and causing a rupture in the whelp. Under-shot mothers are liable to cause the same thing. This need not worry you, for it has no adverse effect on the puppy, whether male or female either now or in later life. In maturity it may well be inconspicuous but if it appears unsightly a veterinary can deal with it quite simply.

WORMS. Most puppies are infested with Roundworm and this pest needs to be eradicated as soon as possible as it stunts growth. Refer to p. 77 for treatment. Tape worm is an infestation found usually in adult animals, probably not so damaging as Roundworm but inclined to prevent a

C

show dog coming to full bloom. It can be recognised by the tape-like segments of worm which appear in the dog's stools or can be seen adhering to the anus. This parasite is a stubborn one. The normal procedure is to starve the dog. This starves the worm and with the arrival of a strong vermifuge the worm, which has unhooked itself from its intestinal nest in search of food, is emitted through the anus.

It is important that all worms should be removed immediately as they are capable of infestation and carry millions of eggs.

CHAPTER SEVEN

Breeding

NOTHING is more satisfying to a doggy enthusiast than to breed a good one! Some people, more fortunate than others, hit the 'jack-pot' and produce a winner with their first try. One man I know, purchased his bitch as a pet, then decided for the sake of the animal's health to breed from her. She produced five puppies, four dogs and a bitch and every one became a noted winner and big name in the show world! Perhaps another breeder might try for years, spending much time and money in his efforts to produce a 'flyer' — all to no avail. There is little doubt that luck must play some part in the game, but then one cannot wait indefinitely for this — success needs hard work too!

To tackle the subject of breeding with some hopes of success you need first to know your breed Standard. Once you know it, you need to understand it before you can apply it to your advantage. As I have shown in earlier pages, an interpretation of the Standard is an individual understanding for whereas it may describe the Perfect Staffordshire Bull Terrier it can be only a guide to a judge. Take your thoughts on the Standard then to a dog show which caters for the best dogs and see how *your* interpretation fits what you see in the best Staffordshire Bull Terriers present. If you make a point of attending the major championship shows to do this, you will have the chance of seeing many of the leading show winners. Some may be champions, dogs which by their excellence have won at least three Best of Sex awards under different judges at the premier shows. You should seek out such fine specimens and examine them

— get your eye full of them, so to speak. You will find that most owners of these dogs are helpful people and will not resent your close interest. In fact, most of them will be only too pleased to talk about their exhibits.

When you are out to learn a subject such as this, apart from reading, few systems prove so effective as watching and listening. Put yourself at the ringside where Staffordshire Bull Terriers are being judged. Have the catalogue for reference, a pencil and paper ready for use. Watch the dogs enter the ring to be judged. Follow each exhibit with your eyes and study his points according to the Standard as well as his individual type. Assess his balance and his movement as he traverses the ring. See how he responds to the atmosphere of the show and his handler and the way he uses his ears and eyes when the judge attracts his attention. Do not wait for the judge to make his placings — jot down on paper how you would yourself make the awards were you judging them — and give your reasons. Obviously, you are at some disadvantage in not being able to handle the animals and for this reason alone you may well find considerable divergence in the official placings and your own forecast. This is not so important as the fact that you have given your mind a valuable exercise and you have been learning by watching. You are going to put these observations to good effect at a later date. With the judging over, take yourself round to the benches where the dogs are. There they are open to public viewing and you are entitled to stare at them if you wish, but it is unwise to handle them without the owners' permission. However, there should be no difficulty in finding out exactly what you wish, most exhibitors being enthusiasts and glad to discuss the merits of their dogs — some only too ready to point out the demerits, imaginary or otherwise of rival dogs! However, whatever is said, you should listen. You do not have to believe it all and you will learn speedily when to start separating the wheat from the chaff! Try to confine your intake of knowledge from people whose own knowledge is factual and who have proved their worth in the breed either by successful breeding and exhibiting or by virtue of their close and intelligent appreciation of the Staffordshire Bull Terrier. You will soon get to know whose opinion has value as well as those whose comments can be taken with the proverbial pinch of salt.

When you arrive at the stage when you wish to choose a mate for your bitch you will need to do some careful thinking. Rearing her and exercising her into the lovely animal she now is has taken a deal of work. You are aware she is a pretty fair specimen and that her breeding is such that she might reasonably produce, when mated to the right dog, something really good. Thus, you do not want to do anything but the right thing. Your interest in the breed may have taken you as a visitor to private kennels. Discussion and show-going will have revealed that many of the young winners being exhibited were sired by a certain stud dog. You may have seen this paragon and admired him. Weighing up his breeding with that of your bitch you may consider him a good mate for her, but you want to be sure. He has a great head and skull. His body is powerfully constructed and he seems to have the right breed temperament but his ears are just that bit untidy. You take a look at your bitch and her ears are hardly her fortune either! You feel then, that in spite of everything, such a union might be unwise. In such a thought you are right and although a breeder can be too careful in his choice of sire it is incumbent upon him for the good of the breed if not for his own satisfaction and the success of his work to go to endless pains to ensure that no two animals with similar faults be brought into union. There seems little sense in 'fixing' a common fault, which is what you would do in the offspring of such a mating. Much better to look around for a dog of suitable breeding as near to good as is the untidy-eared one, but with good ears. Once you have him and being satisfied on all points, go ahead and breed. At least, in the progeny you would be lessening by half the chance of bad ears. Remember, do not rush to champions just because they are champions. Often they are incapable of passing on their own great type and qualities. You can often be clever by seeking out his un-exhibited full litter brother, sometimes a better dog, sometimes not, but often the one to sire the quality stock which is in the blood to give.

A bitch is normally ripe for mating twelve days following the day she first shows colour. Guarded carefully up to this point she can now be introduced to the chosen dog. Some bitches will receive a dog without a murmur — others will start ructions at once. If you have the former type you are fortunate and you can more or less leave matters to take a natural course, provided you keep an eye on things to see the mating through to its satisfactory conclusion. If the dog you use is an experienced one it is unlikely you will be needed there. If he is virtually un-tried at stud, then odd though it may seem, he may not be sure at which end to start and you will need to position him at times. At the moment the dog makes entry he may need to be held there momentarily so that a 'tie' can be effected. This will indicate copulation and may last twenty to thirty minutes, after which the pair will break away from each other; the bitch should then be removed from the scene and the dog allowed a few quiet moments to retract.

If you did not worm your bitch as a precautionary measure just prior to having her mated, you should do so not more than one week following the end of her season. Sixty-three days is the accepted time for a bitch to carry her puppies, but you should be prepared for their earlier arrival — perhaps to the extent of even three or four days. Be watchful however, if the date of delivery goes beyond the date you had in mind for this may indicate complications and it will be as well to consult your vet for his opinion.

Correct exercising during her time — any reduction of her normal quota is an unwise policy. She can have a couple of brisk walks daily, each of about thirty minutes duration. This can be continued up to a fortnight before she is due to whelp when the walks can be slowed up a bit. Boisterous play and jumping about must not be allowed but the exercise should be sufficient to keep her in hard trim, for a slack-muscled bitch does not make a reliable whelper.

Right from the time when she has been mated her feeding should be stepped up — gradually increase her meat ration and see that plenty of milk is included in her diet. Extra nourishment in the form of vitamins daily, such as calcium, cod-liver oil, etc. is essential in laying good foundations for development in the puppies. Be careful that in your enthusiasm to do right by your bitch you do not make her fat and podgy. Try and avoid any atmosphere of nervous anticipation in the home. If your bitch is having her first litter she may be feeling a little odd and apprehension is speedily transmitted from humans to animals. In effect, treat the whole event as a normal happening and you will find your bitch will do the same.

When the bitch begins to whelp she will begin to scratch in labour and keep turning in an effort to position herself comfortably for delivery. At this stage, you or another person whom she likes and trusts should be on hand to supervise the event. If she appears to dislike your attentions — bitches frequently take on an entirely different character at such times — it will be as well to leave her alone, provided you are sufficiently near at hand to cope with any emergency. You will have provided suitable quarters for her to have her puppies in. The whelping box, of good practical design with sufficient room for its purpose, should have been introduced to the bitch for sleeping at least two weeks before she is due to whelp so that she has become used to it. No bedding should be allowed in the box or at most, some disinfected hessian can be introduced so long as it is tacked down securely. Whelps have a nasty habit of wriggling under bedding and out of sight, to be suffocated or sat upon by a clumsy maiden bitch. Never use hay or straw for the same reason.

Your veterinary surgeon should have been fore-warned of the happy event, so that he is ready should he receive your urgent call for assistance. If you are nervy and feel that your worries are likely to be transmitted to the bitch, as does happen at such times, keep away from the scene and leave emergencies to a reliable friend. There is unlikely to be any difficulties — the breed is pretty easy whelping and complications seldom occur. However, just in case assistance is needed prepare yourself with a small First Aid pack, a pair of sterilized surgical scissors, some towelling and what disinfectant you consider necessary. Probably your only task would be to sever the umbilical cord if the bitch failed to do so herself. Briefly, what happens is this — the puppies are born one after the other with varying intervals between each arrival. They usually come out head first, occasionally tail first. This may not cause any distress in the bitch and you should not interfere with things or attempt any assistance unless it is obvious the bitch needs you. In this case the projecting puppy can be gently gripped with a piece of clean towelling and eased out carefully in rhythm with the mother's labour. The bitch should release the puppy from its protective sac herself, nip the umbilical cord and clean up. If she avoids doing any or all of these tasks as sometimes happens with a maiden bitch, you will have to attend to them. Afterbirth follows each puppy and you need have no worries if you see the bitch eat this — in the wild state a female uses it for sustenance during her enforced confinement. Puppies arrive in fairly quick succession and it is as well to check that the final puppy is followed by its afterbirth. After whelping is complete, try and get the bitch outside to relieve herself. If you get the chance during this excursion, clean up the box and make a swift check on the puppies to determine their sex and for any abnormalities. Puppies start feeding at once and will find their own way to their mother's teats. Sometimes the bitch has a slight temperature during her efforts and the milk does not come through at once. However, this subsides quickly and a happy, contented family will be before you. Remember the groin or inguinal teats carry the greatest supply of milk so it is a good idea to ensure that this choice position is fairly shared out among the youngsters.

Keep the bedding nailed down at least for three weeks, but change it for clean at regular and necessary intervals. Do not handle the puppies more than is absolutely essential. Keep children away from them for a while and do not allow strangers in to see them until you are certain the bitch is completely composed with her brood.

Temperament

Perpetuation of correct temperament in the Staffordshire Bull Terrier remains a problem. In the old days of fighting dogs, gameness was essential — only those dogs who possessed it survived or at least finally gave up their lives with full honours. A breeding programme in those days demanded proper temperament as the main attribute in the choice of a sire or a bitch to produce puppies. The make and shape of the parents mattered very little. To-day, too many breeders disregard character and Staffordshire temperament and this is a pity, for although dog pits are virtually non-existent, their influence from the past is not. The joy of owning a Staffordshire Bull Terrier is to savour his temperament to the full. You want a dog completely fearless — nothing embarrasses more than a craven specimen of the breed. You can get away with this if you own a Toy dog, although it must be admitted that many

GESTATION TABLE
Showing when your bitch is due to whelp

MATED JANUARY	DUE TO WHELP MARCH	MATED FEBRUARY	DUE TO WHELP APRIL	MATED MARCH	DUE TO WHELP MAY	MATED APRIL	DUE TO WHELP JUNE	MATED MAY	DUE TO WHELP JULY	MATED JUNE	DUE TO WHELP AUGUST	MATED JULY	DUE TO WHELP SEPTEMBER	MATED AUGUST	DUE TO WHELP OCTOBER	MATED SEPTEMBER	DUE TO WHELP NOVEMBER	MATED OCTOBER	DUE TO WHELP DECEMBER	MATED NOVEMBER	DUE TO WHELP JANUARY	MATED DECEMBER	DUE TO WHELP FEBRUARY
1	5	1	5	1	3	1	3	1	3	1	3	1	2	1	3	1	3	1	3	1	3	1	2
2	6	2	6	2	4	2	4	2	4	2	4	2	3	2	4	2	4	2	4	2	4	2	3
3	7	3	7	3	5	3	5	3	5	3	5	3	4	3	5	3	5	3	5	3	5	3	4
4	8	4	8	4	6	4	6	4	6	4	6	4	5	4	6	4	6	4	6	4	6	4	5
5	9	5	9	5	7	5	7	5	7	5	7	5	6	5	7	5	7	5	7	5	7	5	6
6	10	6	10	6	8	6	8	6	8	6	8	6	7	6	8	6	8	6	8	6	8	6	7
7	11	7	11	7	9	7	9	7	9	7	9	7	8	7	9	7	9	7	9	7	9	7	8
8	12	8	12	8	10	8	10	8	10	8	10	8	9	8	10	8	10	8	10	8	10	8	9
9	13	9	13	9	11	9	11	9	11	9	11	9	10	9	11	9	11	9	11	9	11	9	10
10	14	10	14	10	12	10	12	10	12	10	12	10	11	10	12	10	12	10	12	10	12	10	11
11	15	11	15	11	13	11	13	11	13	11	13	11	12	11	13	11	13	11	13	11	13	11	12
12	16	12	16	12	14	12	14	12	14	12	14	12	13	12	14	12	14	12	14	12	14	12	13
13	17	13	17	13	15	13	15	13	15	13	15	13	14	13	15	13	15	13	15	13	15	13	14
14	18	14	18	14	16	14	16	14	16	14	16	14	15	14	16	14	16	14	16	14	16	14	15
15	19	15	19	15	17	15	17	15	17	15	17	15	16	15	17	15	17	15	17	15	17	15	16
16	20	16	20	16	18	16	18	16	18	16	18	16	17	16	18	16	18	16	18	16	18	16	17
17	21	17	21	17	19	17	19	17	19	17	19	17	18	17	19	17	19	17	19	17	19	17	18
18	22	18	22	18	20	18	20	18	20	18	20	18	19	18	20	18	20	18	20	18	20	18	19
19	23	19	23	19	21	19	21	19	21	19	21	19	20	19	21	19	21	19	21	19	21	19	20
20	24	20	24	20	22	20	22	20	22	20	22	20	21	20	22	20	22	20	22	20	22	20	21
21	25	21	25	21	23	21	23	21	23	21	23	21	22	21	23	21	23	21	23	21	23	21	22
22	26	22	26	22	24	22	24	22	24	22	24	22	23	22	24	22	24	22	24	22	24	22	23
23	27	23	27	23	25	23	25	23	25	23	25	23	24	23	25	23	25	23	25	23	25	23	24
24	28	24	28	24	26	24	26	24	26	24	26	24	25	24	26	24	26	24	26	24	26	24	25
25	29	25	29	25	27	25	27	25	27	25	27	25	26	25	27	25	27	25	27	25	27	25	26
26	30	26	30	26	28	26	28	26	28	26	28	26	27	26	28	26	28	26	28	26	28	26	27
27	31	27	May 1	27	29	27	29	27	29	27	29	27	28	27	29	27	29	27	29	27	29	27	28
28	Apl. 1	28	2	28	30	28	30	28	30	28	30	28	29	28	30	28	30	28	30	28	30	28	Mar 1
29	2	29	3	29	31	29	July 1	29	31	29	31	29	30	29	31	29	Dec 1	29	31	29	31	29	2
30	3	—	—	30	June 1	30	2	30	Aug 1	30	Sept 1	30	Oct 1	30	Nov 1	30	2	30	Jan 1	30	Feb 1	30	3
31	4	—	—	31	2	—	—	31	2	—	—	31	2	31	2	—	—	31	2	—	—	31	4

of these are game little animals. However, one cannot stomach it in a Stafford which is supposed to be a fighting dog, even if you never fight him.

Breeders are requested to watch for correct temperament in their selection of a stud dog. It is an important asset which must be considered in every breeding programme. If the Staffordshire loses this prized ingredient his future in the popularity stakes is doubtful indeed.

CHAPTER EIGHT

Growing Up

Weaning

You can commence weaning Staffordshire Bull Terrier puppies about four days after they are three weeks of age. By this time they will be ready to try food more substantial than the mother's milk and the bitch herself will almost certainly be grateful for some respite from the insatiable appetites. There are a number of first class proprietary milk foods on the market, 'Lactol' and 'Ostermilk' being two well-known sorts. These should be warmed to blood heat and each puppy introduced to its initial taste in turn. You may find it necessary to dip your finger in the milk and let the puppy lap off that, but I have never found any Staffordshire Bull Terrier puppy backward in taking nourishment and the puppies will soon be lapping freely. Once the puppies have taken to this new method you can introduce them to some meat within a few days. This should be of prime quality and finely shredded. It should be fed raw to get the best from it. You should remember too, at this stage when you feed the mother, to feed her smaller cubes of meat than normally. She is liable to disgorge all or part of her meal in her own efforts to aid the weaning process and you need not be alarmed if she does so — it is a quite natural function. If you give her adult-sized pieces of meat and she vomits these then one or more of the greedier puppies may well come into difficulty when trying to eat the offering. The puppies can be given an alternative to meat with lightly boiled milk puddings, poached egg, or even a little minced tripe. In fact, the more you can vary the food, so long as it is legitimate for puppies, the better. Try never to use horse-flesh or animal feeding meats for young puppies. If you have to, then boil it — never feed it raw. From the age when you start weaning the youngsters up to six weeks of age you should increase the number of meals each day so that by the time they are ready to start out in the world alone, they should be on five well spaced meals daily. Let the puppies feed en masse if you have a feeding tray large enough to accommodate them and provided the litter does not have a big bully which tries to hog the lot! Only feed a puppy individually in exceptional circumstances, for one so treated is inclined to prove choosey. When you are trying to build up lusty youngsters a finicky one is a nuisance.

Your bitch will probably have had enough of her brood by the time it is five weeks old. In any case she should be seeing little of the puppies at this stage. They should be feeding quite independently of her and she should be doing no more than to make the occasional tour of inspection in their pen. Maybe these incursions will prove useful in disposing of her remaining milk supplies, although the sooner she is left alone in this respect the quicker she will dry up and regain her figure.

Worming

You will probably see whether the puppies have worms without having to guess. Sometimes they pass them either with faeces or in severe cases through the mouth. You may see a puppy 'tobogganing' its rear end along the ground or giving a sharp squeak at the same time jerking round to its tail in obvious discomfort. If you observe such evidence then it is time to worm them. If they are five weeks of age or less consult your veterinary surgeon for the remedy is one which needs to be prescribed. If the puppies are older then Bob Martin's 'Destrox-Minor' obtainable from your chemist can be used in your own home with safety and good effect. These days worming medicine can be used without the traditional method of initial starving. You should keep an eye open for the round worms, when they are passed — remove these at once and disinfect the immediate area.

Selling

You may have decided to retain one of the puppies and dispose of the rest. This decision you will have taken, no doubt, with some misgivings — if it is your first home-bred litter. Many people so situated, fall in love with their puppies and hate to part with them. There is no doubt about it — small puppies can be most endearing and a source of great interest and amusement in the household. However, keep them too long and you will soon change your mind, for a pack of untrained, bullet-hard Staffords running amok about the place is no fun, even for the most ardent lover of the breed! You should have made your plans for disposing of the puppies at least by the time they have reached five weeks of age. You have, in effect, two ways open to you. You can dispose of them together, as a litter, to a reputable breed kennel. I say breed kennel, rather than a general kennel, for the former may well pay you more and would certainly understand better the handling of its specialised breed. Such a kennel would doubtless have enquiries for stock which it could not fill from its home-bred supplies, and would be pleased to take yours and to ensure they went to good homes. Your second method of disposal would be to advertise them yourself and to sell them to individual customers. If you adopt the first method you may not get quite as much money for them (although this is not always the case), but you will dispense with the headaches of private selling. You will also save a goodly sum by not having to advertise, not having to pay heavy freight and insurance charges in despatch as well as other necessary costs. Neither would you have to cope with a lot of after-sales queries from the buyers on points which you may not feel competent to answer correctly.

Advertising

When advertising, you will have to make your choice for a medium between the specialist dog journals or the lay press. *Dog World* and *Our Dogs* are the two principle papers devoted to the subject and both produce good results. Your local paper will prove much cheaper to advertise in and you may well find it effective if your selling prices are modest. Advertise concisely and effectively. For example, in the local paper you could insert in the appropriate column:

> Pedigree Staffordshire Bull Terrier puppies,
> ready now. Kennel Club registered parents;
> Champion sire. Sound, healthy. Reasonable
> prices to good homes.

followed by your name and address, etc. Such an advertisement would cost very little and you can add to it according to your fancy. Do not advertise the puppies until they are actually ready to go. People who have made up their minds to buy a puppy are not normally patient and you will find that they will expect to take one away with them if they buy it. If you advertise in a dog paper you should really amplify the announcement, perhaps giving the names of the sire and dam of the puppies and strain or show wins and so on. The readers of these magazines recognise such information, contrary to the readers of local papers, and base their interest in stock upon such facts.

Try at all times, in fairness to your puppies, to ensure they end up in good homes. Avoid the family with a batch of untrained children between the ages of one and nine. The parents may well not be aware of the cruelties which could be perpetrated upon an innocent puppy in such a menage. In such homes puppies, even expensive ones, are frequently treated like toys and discarded like them when their novelty has worn off. Neither should you sell to elderly people who cannot give the dog adequate exercise and in any case, may well find a Staffordshire too boisterous. You might ask how on earth you can find out about such things. If the people are local, it is easy enough – you can procrastinate a little when they enquire then look in on them to 'discuss' the matter. It is not difficult to turn the decision into a polite refusal if you find them unsuitable. If they are at a distance and write to you for a puppy, do not be afraid to ask them outright how the dog will live and with whom. If they do not see the concern for the dog's welfare within your questions, then it does not matter whether they buy the puppy or not.

Lastly, view with some doubt the people who have never had a dog before and live in a 'lovely' home. A dog seldom finds a good home in this environment. Hemmed in with 'do's' and 'don'ts' he leads a miserable life himself and contributes nothing to the pleasure of his owners

Discipline

No Staffordshire Bull Terrier should be spoiled and allowed to have his own way. His ebullient outlook on life will encourage him to take full advantage of everything. However, you must train him right from the outset – discipline is essential. Do not be afraid to slap him – his well upholstered cheek muscle is a safe enough place – if he deserves it. He will not feel much and may well believe you are patting him! But you must make him know when you are displeased and he must be made to obey. If you start him off early like this you will have a happier time together. If you leave the training and discipline until later, just because you think all the doggy pranks and boisterousness is amusing, you may regret it. Delay will mean that it becomes far more difficult to break the bad habits and at this point you will find co-existence with your dog not so satisfying. Training always reflects on the owner – if you have a badly trained animal, it may well be your fault, not his! For advice on elementary Obedience Training, read the section on page 47.

Despatch

Try and sell your puppies to people who can collect them or within reasonable delivery distance from your home. You will then have the opportunity of seeing them when they mature and assessing your prowess as a breeder. Further, you will be freed from railway freight expenses, which are considerable and the worries associated with sending livestock far afield, although it must be fairly stated I have found excellent service from British Railways. Added to these anxieties will be the fact that you may live miles from the nearest main line station with poor transport facilities. However, if you have to send one off, obtain a good sized box, allowing the puppy plenty of head room when in a standing position. The girth of the box should be about twice the length of the animal and bedding should be a liberal supply of clean wood wool, obtained from your local greengrocer. Make sure the box is labelled correctly and that your writing is clear. Try and enclose the box as much as possible without interfering with adequate ventilation. A puppy travels better in such a container than in one with say a wire-netting top through which he can see all that is going on. Do not feed him or give even a drink at least two hours before he travels. He will enjoy his trip much better and with greater comfort if you observe this hard-sounding rule. You will have to complete the usual form at the Passenger Parcels Office so allow yourself a good half-hour before the train leaves and make sure his box is put on the stated train before you leave. Your customer should have a complete understanding of the arrangements, day and time of sending. departure station, arrival station and arrival time. Given all these things everything should go like clockwork, but it is good for one's peace of mind if you can arrange between you a telephone call the same evening to ensure the puppy's safe arrival.

Documents

A normal sale of a pedigree puppy entails the supply, by the vendor, of a signed pedigree at least to three generations of the puppy's forebears. If for any reason at all, you cannot complete a pedigree, e.g. maybe the breeding of one parent is unknown or you have mislaid some papers then this fact should have been conveyed to the purchaser at the time. This is assuming that he has paid a proper price for the puppy and is expecting a pedigree, not if he has bought it cheap because of its doubtful antecedents. Many new owners will wish to register their dogs at The Kennel Club, which has headquarters at 1 – 4 Clarges Street, Piccadilly, London, W.1. From there you will be able to obtain the special form 1A which must be used by the new owner after you have completed it and signed it as breeder.

One word of warning — before you send a puppy away, make sure you have payment for it. Some folk are very slow paying after they have the goods. Naturally, a purchaser at a distance will require to see what he is buying before he confirms payment. This is fair enough and you can come to an arrangement with him that you are sending the puppy on approval to him against his remittance, which you require in hand first.

CHAPTER NINE

Exhibiting

THE DOG SHOW ring can prove a most interesting place for the owner of a good pedigree dog. Mind you, if you take loosing badly or think that your ordinary looking specimen is an outstanding champion or start boasting when you get a Highly Commended — then it might be best if you gave up the idea before you started! If on the other hand, you admire the Staffordshire Bull Terrier breed — think it has a future and want to see it progress along correct lines — these commendable attributes being coupled with an ability to lose in fair or foul competition, then by all means enter Dogdom.

You can learn all about forthcoming shows by taking the weekly journals which deal with doggy matters — *Dog World* and *Our Dogs*. In the appropriate columns you will see details of all the local shows and events where Staffordshires are to be classified. You apply to the Secretary (usually honorary) and in due course a schedule arrives through your letter box. You will observe that entries have to be in by a certain closing date, usually from ten to thirty days before the show, according to the type of show. The entry form is self explanatory and you fill in the details of your breed — the dog's name, its sex, date of birth, parentage and the classes in which you wish to enter. The Schedule will explain the merits of these classes and your eligibility. Fees vary and you may have to become a member of some of these dog clubs before you can exhibit at their shows. Of course, your dog or bitch must be registered at The Kennel Club before you can exhibit it at *any* show.

When the day comes along for the show you make sure your exhibit looks good and off you go. Before you can enter the hall to show your dog you will have to let your dog pass a brief veterinary inspection. This prevents sick dogs from entering and passing on their sickness to other dogs. Dogs with skin trouble would be refused entrance too as would monorchids and cryptorchids – male dogs with genital abnormalities, ostracised by The Kennel Club.

Once in the hall it is up to you to keep your eyes and ears open for the steward who will be in the ring with the judge. He will call out the classes and your number when the time comes. You will find your number in the catalogue which you will have purchased at the door and on hearing the call you will enter the ring, receive a number card which you pin to your coat lapel or dress. There is no need to start worrying at this stage. It is all quite simple and even though the ringside might be crowded it is doubtful if anyone is staring at you. Dog show people are more interested in the dogs and musing upon the judge's placings. You just stand there in a line making the best of your dog. The dog, by the way, should be standing on his four feet, not sitting down. He should look alert, intelligent and interested in the proceedings. If he is showing off a bit and taking heed of a neighbouring dog do not stop him unless he really is being a nuisance. It is probable that he is looking good and that is the effect you want. In due course, the judge will call you over to him. He will ask you the age of your dog, probably look at the animals teeth, give it a few prods and feel its contours here and there and ask you to move it away from him. This means you walk it to the other end of the ring and he will then assess how it moves from behind. Then you should turn right around and walk back to him – he will then be assessing the dog's forward movement. One more glance at it and you will be directed back to your previous position in the line.

Once the judge has done this routine with every one in the class he will walk up and down making up his mind which exhibits he is going to pull out for the prizes. If he calls you out first this does not necessarily mean you are to take the red card (first prize) so do not exult at once. He may pick out all those to whom he is going to give prizes then arrange them into position afterwards. He might pick out five dogs he likes better than the others present. He will place them 1, 2, 3 — these being the main prize winners, No. 2 getting a blue card, No. 3 a yellow and then a green card for 'Reserve' which is a sort of fourth prize. There are 'consolation' cards available at some shows — these are termed V.H.C. (Very Highly Commended) and H.C. (Highly Commended). They do not mean very much but they give pleasure to some exhibitors who feel that their dog has not been overlooked. The 'Reserve' card referred to and those such as the V.H.C. and H.C. seldom carry any monetary consideration, although in some cases the winners of these awards receive token prizes such as a packet of dog biscuits or a proprietary medicine, etc. In any case, apart from prizes in stake classes at the major championship shows, which can be substantial — the prizes at local shows are seldom worth much money-wise. However, they are esteemed by seekers after prestige for their dogs. For this reason they are collected, often quite avidly and they frequently prove useful, especially to stud dogs who have won them for they enhance their worth.

It is as well if you win a prize at your first show with the dog not to get too excited about it. There is no harm in being pleased with the success but one judge's opinion is not conclusive as to the show value of your dog. The next time you take him to a show he might meet stronger competition — he might meet a judge who knows the breed well and finds him lacking in certain points. On the other hand, you might well have a good one and your winning ways with the dog will continue. Given genuine encouragement and with an ability to appreciate a dog's points and understand the assessment of them and the general run of the dog game you are in for an enjoyable time. The main thing is to keep a sense of proportion. Too many doggy people go the whole hog — they load themselves and their family with far too many dogs — many of the creatures far from good specimens — all requiring food and attention of course and yet not able to contribute to the advancement of the exhibitor or to the breed in general.

Complete list of Staffordshire Bull Terrier Champions 1939-63

Compiled by C. A. Smith, Esq.

A. DOGS

Name	Sire	Dam
1939		
Ch. Gentleman Jim	Brindle Mick	Triton Judy
Ch. Game Laddie	Game Lad	Mad Molly
1947		
Ch. Head Lad of Villmar	Vindictive Monty of Wyncroft	Fred's Fancy
Ch. Widneyland Kim	Ch. Gentleman Jim	Game Judy
1948		
Ch. Fearless Red of Bandits	Ch. Gentleman Jim	Dees Pegg
Ch. Wychbury Kimbo	Ch. Widneyland Kim	Wychbury Peggy
Ch. Sandra's Boy	Bomber Command	Crossguns Sandra
1949		
Ch. Monty the Monarch	Black Bottle	Willowmay
Ch. Brigands Red Rogerson	Jolly Roger	Lady Juror
Ch. Brindle Mac	Boy Dan	Our Cissy
Ch. Brigands Bosun	Brindle Bill	Fredancer
Ch. Jims Double of Wychbury	Ch. Gentleman Jim	Brindle Trix
Ch. Quiz of Wyncroft	Jolly Roger	Gamesters Hot Black
Ch. Brindle Cresendo of Wychbury	Walters Gift	Brins Best
Ch. Thornhills Pride	Ch. Brigands Bosun	Clipper of Bodenham
1950		
Ch. Wychbury Kimson	Ch. Widneyland Kim	Cradley Janet of Wychbury
Ch. Constones Cadet	Ch. Godfrey's Pride	Constant Coquette
Ch. Peter the Bomber	Bomber Command	Pat's The Girl
Ch. Godfrey's Pride	Ch. Widneyland Kim	Empress Theodora
1951		
Ch. Goldwyns Leading Lad	Wheatley Lad	Brindle Diana
Ch. Red Atom Bomber	Bomber Command	Blackies Girl
Ch. Widneyland Little Gent of Pynedale	Ch. Wychbury Kimbo	Pal O'Derek

Name	Sire	Dam
Ch. Gillcroft Guardson	Milkern Guardson	Lady Patikin
Ch. Emden Corsican	Jolly Roger	Emden Clipper
Ch. Tearaway Rover	Son O' Chall	Troublesome Lass
1952		
Ch. Pal of Aveth	Ch. Quiz of Wyncroft	Elegant Girl
Ch. Chestonion Annoyance	Brigands Benbrook Pirate	Beautiful Black Jane
Ch. Fredan Fireworks	Sans Cooper	Perfect Nance
Ch. Wychbury Diamond King	Diamond Bill	Granby Lass
Ch. Constones Ballyhill Bruce	Idol Bruce	Idol Jill
1953		
Ch. Wardonian Corniche	Ch. Chestonion Annoyance	Wardonian Cintra
Ch. Hillside Toby	Wishbone Willie	Bourhill Lass
Ch. Mahogany Democrat	Brinstock Democrat	Destructive Meg
1954		
Ch. Godella's Pride	Ch. Godfrey's Pride	Ch. Della of Impkin
Ch. Corsair of Wyncole	Jolly Roger	Game Lady of Wyncroft
Ch. Chestonion Satans Fireworks	Ch. Fredan Fireworks	Barrs Road Pride
Ch. Wychbury Red Riband	Ch. Wychbury Kimbo	Regnant Show Lady
Ch. Gentleman Bruce	Crippsian Brindle	Gentle Lady
Ch. Wychbury Sportsman	Ch. Widneyland Kim	Primrose Nance
Ch. Bellerophon Billy Boy	Ch. Quiz of Wyncroft	Honest Martha Le Loop
Ch. Major in Command of Wychbury	Ch. Wychbury Diamond King	Ch. Little Brindle Queen
Ch. Subtle Difference	Ch. Widneyland Kim	Model Miss
Ch. Troglodyte	Ch. Constones Cadet	Monkswood Menace
Ch. Challenger of Dugarde	Bosun of Dugarde	Peggy of Dugarde
1956		
Ch. Golden Boy of Essira	Ch. Goldwyns Leading Lad	Titian of Essira
Ch. Aphonic True Pal	Ch. Hillside Toby	Firey Lass
1957		
Ch. Eastaff Danom	Ch. Goldwyns Leading Lad	Ch. Linda of Killyglen
Ch. Peter's Boy	Ch. Peter the Bomber	Brinstock Game 'Un
Ch. Son of Billy Boy	Ch. Bellerophon Billy Boy	Little Nip
Ch. Dellveth's Pride	Ch. Pal of Aveth, CD. Ex.	Dellfrey's Pride

Name	*Sire*	*Dam*
Ch. Constones Eastaff This'll'do	Ch. Troglodyte	Jill of Prested
1958		
Ch. Toro	Ch. Wychbury Diamond King	Lady Lesette
Ch. The Red Brickmaker	Ch. Wychbury Red Riband	Bilvick Fawn Vixen
Ch. Harwyns Choice	Kim the Duke	Bill's Baby
Ch. Brinstock Glenagow	Ch. Dellveth's Pride	Ch. Brinstock Welsh Maid
1959		
Ch. Iron Bill of Phylmajar	Ch. Peters Boy	Tinkerbelle Susan
Ch. Weycombe Dandy	Ch. Golden Boy of Essira	Ch. Weycombe Cherry
Ch. Buster Bill	Ch. Bellerophon Billy Boy	Bowbrooke Bess
Ch. Goldwyn Lucky Lad	Ch. Goldwyns Leading Lad	Ch. Goldwyns Gracious Lady
Ch. Rellim A'boy	Ch. Wychbury Red Riband	Ch. Wychbury Midly Girl
1960		
Ch. Sahib of Senkrah	Ch. Eastaff Danom	Ch. Weycombe Julie
1961		
Ch. Top Hat	Ch. Bellerophon Billy Boy	Ruf-E-Nuf of Fulstone
Ch. Chestonion Campaign	Ch. Son of Billy Boy	Maid of Kinderlee
Ch. The Prince of Diamonds	Ch. Major in Command of Wychbury	Lady Flossie of Uddfa
1962		
Ch. Rellim Ferryvale Victor	Ch. Rellim A'boy	Chestonion Chimes
Ch. Wynchal Buckeroo	Ch. Son of Billy Boy	Stanwall Cheeky Charlotte
1963		
Ch. The Black Monarch	Black King	Atom Choice
Ch. Jolihem Fine and Dandy	Jolihem Adonis	Black Fury
Ch. Weycombe Benny	Weycombe Timothy	Weycombe Beauty
Ch. Bandits Brintiga	Georgecrofts Mandumas	Satan's Mistress
Ch. Bandits Red Armour	Weycombe Gerard	Jill of Bovinger

B. BITCHES

Name	Sire	Dam
1939		
Ch. Lady Eve	Barney	Gipsy
Ch. Midnight Gift	Game Bill	Blue Bell Bess
Ch. Madcap Mischief	Ch. Game Laddie	Timyke Mustard
1947		
Ch. Widneyland Model	Togo	White Bess
Ch. Wychbury Red Cap	Ch. Brigands Bosun	Rita's Pride
1948		
Ch. Wychbury Oak Beauty	Prince St. John	Vindictive Flirt
Ch. Widneyland Ritver Ringleader	Ch. Brigands Bosun	Uta of Roxana
Ch. Perfect Lady	Furnace Jake	Plucy Queen
1949		
Ch. Brinstock Sandy Bridget	Ch. Game Laddie	Brinstock Bridget
Ch. Our Queenie	Tigers the Boy	Bombshell Judy
Ch. Wychbury Pied Wonder	Ch. Widneyland Kim	Christie of Wyncroft
Ch. Lucky Star of Bandits	Bucks Mick	Lucy's Luce
Ch. Eastbury Lass	Ch. Gentleman Jim	Invincible Belle
1950		
Ch. Nuneato Dinah	Nuneatonion Boy	Lady Shan
Ch. Tawney of Dugarde	Ch. Sandra's Boy	Jezebel of Dugarde
Ch. Brinstock Red Radiance	Ch. Game Laddie	Red Sadie
Ch. Della of Impkin	Ch. Widneyland Kim	Christie of Wyncroft
1951		
Ch. Widneyland Panda	Widneyland Little Patch	Brindle Daisy
Ch. Nita's Choice	Tenacious Pete	Blandona Black Queen
Ch. Tessa's Gem	Ch. Wychbury Kimbo	Tessa of Burnttree
1952		
Ch. Gwornall Eve	Rambling Knight	Gwornall Britannia
Ch. Linda of Killyglen	Brigands Bosun Beau	Colleen of Killyglen
Ch. Fancy Fay of Summermuir	True Briton	Ch. Our Queenie
Ch. Fredan Blonde Bombshell	Sans Cooper	Perfect Nance

Name	*Sire*	*Dam*
Ch. Lady Cherie of Uddfa	Allan's Dynamo	Felicitus of Nanholme

1953

Ch. Little Brindle Queen	Ch. Widneyland Little Gent of Pynedale	Regency Beauty
Ch. Red Biddy of Zendiks	Brians Choice	October Lady
Ch. Brinstock Welsh Maid	Timothy of Dugarde	Queen of Barry
Ch. Wychbury Midly Girl	Ch. Widneyland Kim	Regnant Show Lady

1954

Ch. Wyngate Lady	Corinthian Rick	Red Demon Lass
Ch. Gwornall Judith	Rambling Knight	Gwornall Britannia
Ch. Emden Cuttysark	Ch. Godella's Pride	Emden Charanda

1955

Ch. Williamwood Golden Lass	Ch. Wychbury Kimbo	Williamwood Wonder Girl
Ch. Tawndiamond of Dugarde	Ch. Wychbury Diamond King	Ch. Tawney of Dugarde
Ch. Fredanseuse	Fredante	Apache Princess
Ch. Linksbury Derry	Ch. Godfrey's Pride	Ch. Nuneato Dinah
Ch. Goldwyns Gracious Lady	Wheatley Lad	Brindle Diana
Ch. Lady of Barnfield	Ch. Thornhills Pride	Freds Lass of Summermuir
Ch. Eastaff Nicola	Ch. Wychbury Kimbo	Ch. Linda of Killyglen

1956

Ch. Weycombe Cherry	Gentleman Jackson	Weycombe Judy
Ch. Wychbury Sporting Girl	Ch. Wychbury Sportsman	Saucy Dinah
Ch. Andra of Towans	Ch. Wychbury Sportsman	Tina of Towans
Ch. Smallthorn Brindle Peggy	Cheirons Black Mike	Lovely Cottage
Ch. Chestonion Elegance	Ch. Chestonion Annoyance	Ch. Freden Blonde Bombshell

1957

Ch. Little Diamond Tiara	Ch. Wychbury Red Riband	Queenie's Dynamite
Ch. Linksbury Amanda	Linksbury Victor	Ch. Linksbury Derry
Ch. Williamwood Fawn Lass	Ch. Wychbury Red Riband	Ch. William Golden Lass
Ch. Bankhead Beauty	Southfield Rufus	Sallys Pride or Mayeswood
Ch. Trenton Tiger Lily	Ch. Goldwyns Leading Lad	Deceptive Dora

Name	Sire	Dam
1958		
Ch. Fiona Beauty	Crown Major	Ch. Gwornal Judith
Ch. Wawocan Benita	Ch. Peters Boy	Little Choice
Ch. Dennybeck Graftwood Tanya	Jupitor of Graftwood	Graftwood Melissande
Ch. Towans Merry Maid	Ch. Wychbury Red Riband	Tina of Towans
1959		
Ch. Moira Meg	Ch. Constones Cadet	Nancie's Pride
Ch. Weycombe Julie	Ch. Golden Boy of Essira	Ch. Weycombe Cherry
Ch. Pitbul Lindy Lou	Ch. Eastaff Danom	Pitbul Amber Queen
Ch. Mandy of Mandalay	Ch. Godella's Pride	Hayward's Flash
1960		
Ch. Stretfordian Little Gem	Stretfordian Lad	Stretfordian Weycombe Trudy
Ch. Fredanita of Wychbury	Ch. Major in Command of Wychbury	Fredansante
Ch. Weycombe Melody of Senkrah	Ch. Golden Boy of Essira	Ch. Weycombe Cherry
Ch. Judy of Brunanburgh	Ch. Bellerophon Billy Boy	Bellerophon Brindle Sue
1961		
Ch. Brindle Ballerina	Ch. Major in Command of Wychbury	Lady Black Beauty
Ch. Yasmin of Beredhar	Ch. Peters Boy	Rivaz of Beredhar
Ch. Gay Moment	Ch. Major in Command of Wychbury	Spring Fury
Ch. Fiery Goddess	Georgecroft Golden Boy	Satans Mistress
1962		
Ch. Jolihem Forclip Christy Bella	Ch. Goldwyns Lucky Lad	Forclip Poor Mary
Ch. Marjories Choice	Ch. Bellerophon Billy Boy	Dorothy's Choice
Ch. Game Penny	Weycombe Shan	Glendover Brindle Beverley
Ch. Fredenzella	Ch. Major in Command of Wychbury	Fredansante
Ch. Vesper Andromeda	Rumbuster	Vesper Countess
1963		
Ch. Senkrah Saffron	Ch. Weycombe Dandy	Senkrah Sabelle
Ch. Stonnards Nell	Ch. Eastaff Danom	Stonnards Imogen
Ch. Senkrah Sapphire	Ch. Weycombe Dandy	Senkrah Sabelle
Ch. Bandits Brindemara	Trenton Colonel	Linksbury Dillyness

APPENDIX TWO

Breed Clubs

THE STAFFORDSHIRE BULL TERRIER CLUB:
Mrs. G. A. Dudley, 'Wychbury House', Swindells Road, Pedmore, Stourbridge, N. Worcs.

*NORTH EASTERN BULL TERRIER AND STAFFORDSHIRE BULL TERRIER CLUB:
G. Clank, Esq., 46 Beatrice Road, Heaton, Newcastle upon Tyne, 6.

*NOTTS AND DERBY DISTRICT BULL TERRIER CLUB:
G. Haynes, 66 Highfield Drive, Nottingham.

NORTHERN COUNTIES STAFFORDSHIRE BULL TERRIER CLUB:
A. H. Eastwood, Esq., 70 Upper Brow Road, Paddock, Huddersfield, Yorks.

EAST MIDLANDS STAFFORDSHIRE BULL TERRIER CLUB:
J. E. Adderson, Esq., Hazelmere, Mere Road, Wigston Magna, Leics.

SOUTHERN COUNTIES STAFFORDSHIRE BULL TERRIER SOCIETY:
Major F. C. Rowley, 7 Clanricarde Gardens, London W.2.

POTTERIES STAFFORDSHIRE BULL TERRIER CLUB:
G. Milward, Esq., 'Rockwoods', Newcastle Road, Ashley Heath, Market Drayton, Salop.

NORTH-WEST STAFFORDSHIRE BULL TERRIER CLUB:
E. J. Bywaters, Esq., 131 Grey Mare Lane, Manchester 11.

NORTHERN IRELAND STAFFORDSHIRE BULL TERRIER CLUB:
J. C. Courtney, Esq., 3 Carrisbrook Gardens, Lambeg, Co. Antrim.

SCOTTISH STAFFORDSHIRE BULL TERRIER CLUB:
F. Gillespie, Esq., 7 Novar Drive, Glasgow W.2.

STAFFORDSHIRE BULL TERRIER CLUB OF IRELAND:
E. Byrne, Esq., 9 Sperrin Road, Drimnagh, Dublin.

* *These clubs cater for the Bull Terrier and the Staffordshire Bull Terrier.*

Index